Gavin Douglas

The Palis of Honoure

Middle English Texts

General Editor

Russell A. Peck
University of Rochester

Advisory Board

Rita Copeland
University of Texas

Thomas G. Hahn
University of Rochester

Lisa Kiser
Ohio State University

Thomas Seiler
Western Michigan University

R. A. Shoaf
University of Florida

Bonnie Wheeler
Southern Methodist University

The Middle English Texts Series is designed for classroom use. Its goal is to make available to teachers and students texts which occupy an important place in the literary and cultural canon but which have not been readily available in student editions. The series does not include those authors such as Chaucer, Gower, Langland, the Pearl-poet, or Malory, whose English works are normally in print in good student editions. The focus is, instead, upon Middle English literature adjacent to those authors that teachers need in compiling the syllabuses they wish to teach. The editions maintain the linguistic integrity of the original work but within the parameters of modern reading conventions. The texts are printed in the modern alphabet and follow the practices of modern capitalization and punctuation. Manuscript abbreviations are expanded, and u/v and j/i spellings are regularized according to modern orthography. Hard words, difficult phrases, and unusual idioms are glossed on the page, either in the right margin or at the foot of the page. Textual notes appear at the end of the text, along with a glossary. The editions include short introductions on the history of the work, its merits and points of topical interest, and also include briefly annotated bibliographies.

Gavin Douglas

The Palis of Honoure

Edited by
David Parkinson

Published for TEAMS
(The Consortium for the Teaching of the Middle Ages)
in Association with the University of Rochester

by

Medieval Institute Publications

WESTERN MICHIGAN UNIVERSITY

Kalamazoo, Michigan — 1992

Library of Congress Cataloging-in-Publication Data

Douglas, Gavin, 1474?-1522.
    The palis of honoure / edited by David Parkinson.
        p. cm. -- (Middle English texts)
    Includes bibliographical references.
    ISBN 1-879288-25-7 (paper)
    I. Parkinson, David John, 1956- . II. Title. III. Series: Middle English texts
(Kalamazoo, Mich.)
    PR2252.P3 1992
    821'.2--dc20   92-32976
                                                                   CIP

ISBN 1-879288-25-7

Copyright 1992 by the Board of the Medieval Institute
Second Printing 2001

Printed in the United States of America

Cover design by Elizabeth King

Contents

Preface

The following edition is offered as a student's introduction to Gavin Douglas's *The Palis of Honoure*, a fascinating but still rather neglected dream poem of early sixteenth-century Scotland. For access to microfilm copies of the sixteenth-century prints of the poem, I am grateful to the British Library, Edinburgh University Library, the Huntington Library, and the National Library of Scotland. The usefulness of this edition will depend to a great extent on how well it has been founded on the wide-ranging and perceptive researches of Priscilla Bawcutt; her edition of *The Palis of Honoure* and her critical study of Douglas have been constantly helpful. That this edition has been attempted at all owes much to the encouragement given by Alasdair MacDonald and Elizabeth Archibald, and to support given by the Editorial Board of this series. Without the wisdom and vigilance of its General Editor, the outcome would have been far poorer than it is. I am grateful to the University of Saskatchewan for a grant used to hire an excellent assistant, Tamara Wiens. Finally, Mary Parkinson has lovingly and perceptively helped me see this edition through.

The Palis of Honoure

Introduction

If he is mentioned at all in studies of late medieval literature, Gavin Douglas tends to appear as the last and least member of a triumvirate of Scots poets, overshadowed by his older compatriots Robert Henryson and William Dunbar. This is unfortunate but understandable. Douglas's major work is *Eneados*, a Scots verse translation of Virgil's *Aeneid*; his only other extant poem of substance, *The Palis of Honoure*, may be regarded as something of a trial run for the larger Virgilian project to come. Still, prejudice against apprentices and translators notwithstanding, Douglas has his own strengths in *The Palis*, as later in *Eneados* — descriptive precision and concreteness, pungency of dialogue and versatility of diction generally, vividness of persona, and keenness of critical response to earlier books and writers. *The Palis of Honoure* may certainly be read for the sense of tradition (literary, but also ethical) which it articulates; and it will continue to impress modern readers by means of its sheer verve and inventiveness.

The Author and the Date of Composition of **The Palis of Honoure**

Gavin Douglas's life seems to divide neatly into two parts, the events of his youth having passed largely unrecorded, while those of his later maturity are documented in some detail. Although he was a younger son of a powerful family in Scotland (his father being Archibald "Bell-the-Cat" Douglas, fifth Earl of Angus), the place and even the date of Douglas's birth are not known: it is likely that he was born at Tantallon Castle in East Lothian (that being the chief residence of the Earl of Angus), probably in 1474 or 1475. Douglas matriculated at St. Andrews University in 1490, and completed his master's degree there in 1494; he may have gone on, as other Scottish students did, to study at Paris. Still, it seems probable that he resided largely in Edinburgh in the later 1490s, during which he was seeking a secure source of income from a Church appointment. After being involved in at least three disputes over the awarding of ecclesiastical offices, Douglas was appointed Provost of the collegiate church of St. Giles, in Edinburgh. This was an office awarded by the king, and Douglas had been installed as Provost by March 1503.

1

Hardly more than a month before the catastrophic Battle of Flodden (9 September 1513), on 22 July 1513, Douglas completed his translation of the *Aeneid*, bringing that work to a close with a farewell to poetry. Ahead lay rapid, brilliant advancement. Douglas was uncle of the sixth Earl of Angus, who, eleven months after the death of King James IV at Flodden, married the widowed Queen, Margaret, sister of Henry VIII of England. Douglas gained eminence, becoming Bishop of Dunkeld in 1516. Hard on the heels of his rise came inevitable hostility; then, with the Douglas faction falling from power, came disfavor and, finally, departure to England, where he died in September 1522.

Douglas's poetry is the product of his relatively obscure youth. *The Palis of Honoure* was completed in 1500 or 1501, during the poet's quest at court for ecclesiastical preferment. (At the end of his *Eneados*, Douglas states that he had finished *The Palis* "weil twelf yheiris" before.) Addressed as it is to King James IV, *The Palis* may be seen as an astute display of its author's eloquence. Indeed, writing this ambitious poem would have been an appropriate way for Gavin Douglas to further his candidacy for an office such as the Provostship of St. Giles.

The Sixteenth-Century Prints of The Palis and the Text of this Edition

No contemporary manuscripts of *The Palis of Honoure* are known to exist. However, there are complete copies extant of two sixteenth-century editions of this poem, along with fragments of a third.

D: Fragments of the first quire (A^4) of a quarto edition printed by Thomas Davidson at Edinburgh, c. 1535 (STC 7072.8), the unique copy of which is housed at Edinburgh University Library.

L: A quarto edition (forty leaves, A–K^4) entitled thus:

> THE / PALIS OF / Honoure Compyled by / Gawyne dowglas Bys- / shope of Dunkyll. / Imprinted at London in / fletstret, at the sygne of / the Rose garland by / wyllyam / Copland. / God saue Quene / Marye.

Given its similarities to Copland's edition of Douglas's translation of the *Aeneid* (*Eneados*, printed 1553), this book has been dated c. 1553 (STC 7073). Nine copies survive; facsimiles of the copies housed at the British Library and the Henry E. Huntington Library have been consulted for the present edition. As the Davidson edition would have done in its perfect state, this edition presents twenty-nine lines of verse per page. Copland's text of *The Palis* is probably derived from a Scottish

2

print similar to Davidson's. A feature of Copland's print is the inclusion of explanatory side-notes, some of which merely name the personage referred to at that juncture in the poem, while others cite a source or provide a gloss. These notes occasionally betray their Scottish origin in their vocabulary and spellings. The more interesting of these notes are included in the Explanatory Notes of the present edition.

E: A quarto edition (again, forty leaves, A–K⁴) entitled thus:

> Heir beginnis / ane Treatise callit the PALICE / of HONOVR, Compylit / be M. GAWINE / DOWGLAS / Bischop of /Dunkeld. / Imprentit at Edin- / burgh be Iohne Ros, / for Henrie Charteris.Anno. 1579. / CUM PRIVILEGIO REGALI.

Two copies of this edition survive, one at the National Library of Scotland in Edinburgh, the other at Edinburgh University Library. A microfilm of the former copy has been consulted for the present edition. This copy has one curious feature: in its margins, it contains some emendations inscribed in a sixteenth-century hand, some of which seem to be derived from a text of the poem close to that of Copland's edition. In a brief preface addressed "To the Reidar," however, the publisher Henry Charteris draws attention to the correctness of his text:

> Quhen we had sene and considderit the divers impressiones befoir imprentit of this notabill werk, to have bene altogidder faultie and corrupt: not onlie thar quhilk hes bene imprentit at London, bot also the copyis set furth of auld amangis our selfis: we have thocht gude to tak sum panes and trawellis to have the samin mair commodiously and correctly set furth: to the intent, that the benevolent reidar may have the mair delyte and plesure in reiding, and the mair frute in perusing the plesand and delectabill werk.

According to Charteris, then, William Copland's London print is hopelessly unreliable. Comparison of the two texts does not suggest that Charteris's print is substantially better, however. To be sure, Copland's text contains several errors, misprints and even misreadings, as well as the glaring omission of a whole stanza (lines 1711–19); but on the other hand, Charteris seems to have been a more thorough editor of the poem, tidying up (and anglicizing) the spelling to conform with late sixteenth-century Scottish practice, and providing contemporary alternatives to obsolete grammatical forms and words preserved in Copland's print. In short, Copland is sloppy but arguably closer to Douglas's original; in those stanzas for which the fragments of Davidson's print preserve evidence, Copland and Davidson tend to agree against Charteris. Copland presents a text in which spelling and vocabulary may reflect early-sixteenth-century Scottish practice more clearly than does Charteris's more carefully-edited text.

The best case for adopting Copland's print as copy-text over Charteris's is the superiority of its readings. In a significant majority of cases where the two prints differ substantively, Copland's can be shown to have the better reading (lines 99, 111, 132, 144, 157, 372, 456, 518, 617, 716, 772, 786, 833, 836, 869, 943, 948–51, 984, 990, 1016, 1026, 1037, 1040, 1048, 1135, 1280, 1327, 1363, 1368, 1373, 1379, 1380, 1498, 1616, 1794, 1856, 1890, 1966, 1972, 1973, 2097, 2118, and 2122). Still, there are a number of spots where a preference is not easy to state with confidence (3, 39, 342, 486, 534, 644, 882, 905, 1150, 1354, 1598, 1721, 1803, and 1921), and some others where the Edinburgh print is superior (613, 1022, 1705, 1711–19 [the stanza omitted by Copland], 1814, 1856).

The basis for the present edition, then, is Copland's print of c. 1553. Obvious misreadings in that print have been replaced by readings from Charteris's print wherever Charteris offers a clear improvement in sense.

There have been five editions of *The Palis of Honoure* since the sixteenth century. The first four of these editions all use the Edinburgh print as copy-text. Bawcutt's edition is particularly useful, with its full introduction, accurate presentation of the texts of all three of the sixteenth-century prints, full recording of press variants and emendations, and excellent notes and glossary. Bawcutt gives primacy to the Edinburgh print, editing it as the reading text (with modernized punctuation). Nevertheless, a strong case for adopting the London text as the basis for an edition develops through Bawcutt's comparisons of individual cases of variation, in the Notes to her edition. Thus the most recent edition of an extract from *The Palis of Honoure*, in Douglas Gray's anthology *The Oxford Book of Late Medieval Verse and Prose* (1985), uses the London print as copy text, while adopting readings from Edinburgh where these are clearly superior (lines 320–23, 477–78).

Language, Versification, and Style

The Palis of Honoure is written in Older Scots, the linguistic descendant of the language (Northumbrian Old English permeated by Old Norse) spoken by the twelfth-century English immigrants to the burghs of southern and eastern Scotland. By the middle of the fifteenth century, this naturalized variety of English had become the dominant language of secular administration (replacing Latin), and was expanding further west and north as the common speech, edging out Gaelic. "Older Scots" refers to the variety of English recorded in Scotland from the earliest occurrences in the twelfth century until the Union of England and Scotland (1707); "Middle Scots" refers to the later phases of Older Scots, from its period of highest prestige and integrity as a national language (1450–1550), into a period of increasing conformity of the written and printed standard with that of southern English (1550–1700).

A brief glance at some aspects of Older Scots spelling and grammatical forms may be useful preparation for a first reading of *The Palis*. Perhaps the most obtrusive feature of Older Scots spelling is the regular occurrence of *quh* for southern English *wh* (e.g., *quhen* for *when*, *quhois* for *whose*; 1, 24); more pervasive is *a* where *o* would be expected (e.g., *na* for *no*, *amang* for *among*, *maist* for *most*; 381, 26, 74). See also, for example, *ch* for *gh* (e.g., *thocht* for *thought*, *sycht* for *sight*; 737, 401); *s* for *sh* (*stonyst* for *astonished*, *onabasitly* for *unabashedly*, *vincus* for *vanquish*, *sall* for *shall*; 1161, 1679, 1685, 168); *-is* (or *-ys*) for *-s* or *-es* (*treis* for *trees*, *brekkis* for *breaks*, *exemplys* for *examples*; 26, 373, 760); *-it* (or *-yt*) for *-ed* (*entrit* for *entered*, *alteryt* for *altered*; 7, 744); *-and* in place of *-ing* for the present participle of the verb (e.g., *rynnand* for *running*, *syngand* for *singing*; 140, 1154).

The language of *The Palis of Honoure* is complicated, however, by stylistic aspirations, this poem being an example of Scots "courtly verse in the grand manner," in which southern English forms may replace Scots ones, often to regulate scansion or rhyme: thus the English *o* can appear instead of the usual *a* (e.g., *stone* for *stane*, *mone* for *mane*; 428, 232); the infinitive and the plural present indicative of the verb are occasionally furnished with the *-ing* inflection (e.g., *obeysyng* for *obey*, *rydyng* for *ride*; 1067, 1253). Auxiliary verbs typical of southern English also crop up: most common among these is *do*, usually a metrical filler or modal intensifier, as is the rarer *couth* (e.g., 840, 925).

In this sort of poetry, certain classes of words, levels of style, and devices of rhetoric occur frequently. The poem is rich — especially so during passages of laudatory description — in latinisms and gallicisms (e.g., *distillant, reparcust, respirature*, and also *amyable* and *dulce*; 16, 25, 66, 5, 15), as well as courtly terms of native origin (e.g., *bewes, garth, meid, glete*; 9, 62, 1140, 843). There is some reliance on a courtly repertory of Chaucerisms (e.g., *from, morowe, tho*, and *twane*; 265, 33, 92, 231). Sentence structure can approach extremes of complexity, sometimes (as in the opening of the poem) across the stanza break. Sometimes, the verse becomes suffused with "colors" of rhetoric: periphrasis, apostrophes, exclamations, and rhetorical questions, often together with anaphora (the repetition over several lines of an initial word or phrase; e.g., 174–81, 627–36, 835–49, 1025–34, 1055–57); also admissions of ignorance or inexpressibility (occupatio; e.g., 387, 1061–62, 1426–27, 1477–80, 1254–66); digression (364–84); antithesis (e.g., 174–81, 601–02); hyperbaton (artificial word-order: e.g., 790–98, 991, 1063–67); and antonomasia (the names of mythological deities — Aurora, Phoebus, Neptune, etc. — given to natural phenomena). These "colors" cluster thickly in passages of description (the "pleasant place";

1–54, 1144–52, 1413–40) and apology (127–35, 2150–69), as well as in the many catalogues (of lovers, musical terms, poets, rivers and mountains, points of architecture, officers of court, and heroes). The ideal of eloquence tends to be one of abundance.

This does not result in an unrelievedly stiff texture, however. Style grows plainer in passages of moral exhortation or instruction (e.g., 1380–1404, 1963–2015), and becomes markedly vernacular in informal dialogue (e.g., 706–26, 1734–48, 1935–58). There is also scope for sudden shifts in style, in passages concerning unpleasant experiences (e.g., 136–62 and 1315–77).

The versification of *The Palis* suits the courtly aspirations of the poem. The Prologue and first two Parts are written in a nine-line stanza (*aabaabbab₅*, the stanza of William Dunbar's *Goldyn Targe* and the Complaint in Chaucer's *Anelida and Arcite*); in the third book a slightly different rhyme scheme is used (*aabaabbcc₅*; the stanza of Chaucer's *Complaint of Mars*). Douglas also inserts "lays" and "ballats" into the poem; two of these are in a ten-line stanza (*aabaabbabb₅*; 607–36; 1015–44; the two which conclude the work return to the rhyme-scheme of the nine-line stanza in Parts One and Two, but complicate it by the addition of rhyme within and across lines. With such demanding rhyme schemes, rhyme-tags (e.g., *bedene, with byssy cure, but weir, God wait*) offer an inviting way out of tight corners. Throughout the poem, the line sticks closely to an iambic, ten-syllable pattern.

Literary Associations

The Palis of Honoure exemplifies the courtly tradition of Older Scots verse. Like Richard Holland's *Buke of the Howlat* (c. 1448) or David Lindsay's *Dreme* (1528), it is an allegorical dream-vision: by describing the education of a not very educable courtier, it presents to a noble personage (in this case, the king himself) a "mirror" of proper comportment. A prince's duties, pastimes, sentiments, ideals, and sense of tradition are expounded, with the uncomprehending dreamer serving as foil to the noble reader for whom the poem is intended. Indeed, the catalogues out of which much of *The Palis of Honoure* is constructed offer the reader lists of entries to a variety of important topics, most significantly, literature, history, and pastime from a courtly perspective (1185–233, 1495–1728); imbedded within *The Palis* is the skeleton of a rather specialized encyclopedia.

The poem is based upon a distinction between earthly and heavenly, the one changeable and untrustworthy, the other worthwhile and permanent. The dream shows a way to approach the heavenly ideal, ascending from a chaotic and infernal beginning. Thus the impressive but tyrannical deities who dominate the First Part of the poem (Venus, Cupid, and Mars) give place to the genuinely harmonizing influence of the Muses (the "kingly" Muse Calliope eminent among them) in the Second Part; then, in the Third Part, a more benevolent Venus is revealed in the precincts of the Palace of Honour, and the god Honour appears to be (among other things) a somewhat moralized version of Mars, the patron of those heroes and heroines who have fought justly.

The identity of this God remains something of a mystery. He bears resemblance to the Christian God, as well as pagan deities such as Apollo, Mars, and Cupid. He judges usurpation and lack of fortitude, which he punishes harshly; he also rewards honorable action with everlasting bliss, but does so for a rather un-Christian congregation of worthy men and women (2017–25). This difficulty is heightened by a peculiar variation in the epithet given him at the moment the dreamer catches a glimpse of him: in L, he is called *armypotent;* in E, *omnipotent.* Perhaps it is wiser not to hurry to resolve the balance between Christian and pagan in the person of Honoure; after all, this is the balance on which the whole poem rests.

The Palis of Honoure can be seen in the midst of a complex of literary antecedents and affiliations. Given the wide interest in the acquisition and duration of genuine honor, it is no surprise to find courtly poems on this topic also being written at this time in France and England by such writers as Octovien Saint-Gelais, Jean Lemaire le Belges, Alexander Barclay, Stephen Hawes, and John Skelton. There are of course important English antecedents, such as John Lydgate's *Temple of Glass* and *Complaint of the Black Knight*, as well as Chaucer's dream-visions, most notably *The House of Fame,* which *The Palis* imitates in a variety of ways. Douglas also owes much to the Roman poets Ovid and Virgil, especially the former, whose *Metamorphoses* provides many of his mythological references. Intermingled with references to classical history, geography, and myth are many Biblical references, Christian doctrine and pagan lore having been assumed to be complementary. *The Palis* is a bookish poem, to be sure; but Douglas generally avoids pedantry by maintaining a close relation between reading (and writing) and progress, spatially considered, towards realization (if not possession) of an ideal. This is a work for which distinctions between "medieval" and "Renaissance" become hard to maintain: the dreamer envisions an invigorating world of learning, but does not seem terribly confident about his own ability to enter and possess it.

A Note on the Presentation of Text in this Edition

The following edition of *The Palis of Honoure* uses William Copland's print (London, c. 1553) as copy-text. The spelling of this print is reproduced, with the following exceptions: thorn (þ) and yogh (ȝ) are transcribed *th* and *y*; and *u, v,* and *w* are redistributed according to modern convention, as are *i* and *j*. Word-division has been regularized without notice. Capitalization is restricted to proper names, and beginnings of lines and sentences; punctuation is provided according to modern convention; abbreviations are silently expanded.

The text is followed by textual notes which record substantive variants between the sixteenth-century prints. A full collation of Copland's text with those of Davidson and Charteris has resulted in the adoption of some readings from the Charteris print. Press variants in the nine extant copies of Copland's print are not recorded.

Bibliography

Abbreviations:
D [Fragments of *The Palis of Honoure*] Edinburgh: Davidson, c. 1535.
E *The Palice of Honour*. Edinburgh: John Ros, for Henry Charteris, 1579.
L *The Palis of Honoure*. London: William Copland, c. 1553.
B *The Shorter Poems of Gavin Douglas*, ed. Priscilla Bawcutt.

Editions

Select Works of Gawin Douglass, Bishop of Dunkeld. [Ed. J. Scott.] Perth: R. Morison, Jr., 1787, pp. 1–88.

Scotish Poems, Reprinted from Scarce Editions. Ed. John Pinkerton. 3 vols. London: J. Nichols, 1792. Rpt. New York: AMS Press, 1976. I, 51–141.

The Palice of Honour By Gawyn Douglas, Bishop of Dunkeld. Ed. J. G. Kinnear. Edinburgh: Bannatyne Club 17 (1827). Rpt. New York: AMS Press, 1971.

The Poetical Works of Gavin Douglas, Bishop of Dunkeld. Ed. John Small. 4 vols. Edinburgh: Paterson, 1874. Rpt. Hildesheim: Georg Olms, 1970. I, 1–82.

The Shorter Poems of Gavin Douglas. Ed. Priscilla Bawcutt. Scottish Text Society 4th series 3 (Edinburgh and London: William Blackwood and Sons, 1967), pp. 1–133. [Parallel texts of L and E, along with the D fragments.]

Introduction

The Palis of Honoure Compyled by Gawayne Dowglas Bysshope of Dunkyll [London 1553]. The English Experience, no. 89. Amsterdam: Theatrum Orbis Terrarum; New York: Da Capo, 1969. [A facsimile edition of the Copland print.]

Studies and Sources

Aitken, A. J. "The Language of Older Scots Poetry." In *Scotland and the Lowland Tongue: Studies in the Language and Literature of Lowland Scotland in Honour of David D. Murison*, ed. J. Derrick McClure (Aberdeen: Aberdeen University Press, 1983), pp. 18–49.

———. "Variational Variety in Written Middle Scots." In *Edinburgh Studies in English and Scots*, ed. A. J. Aitken et al (London: Longman, 1971), pp. 176–209.

Armstrong, Edward A. *Folklore of Birds.* London: Collins, 1958.

The Asloan Manuscript. Ed. W. A. Craigie. 2 vols. Scottish Text Society n.s. 14, 16. Edinburgh: William Blackwood and Sons, 1924–25.

Bawcutt, Priscilla. *Gavin Douglas: A Critical Study.* Edinburgh: Edinburgh University Press, 1976.

———. "Henryson's 'Poeit of the Auld Fassoun.'" *Review of English Studies,* n.s. 32 (1981), 429–34.

———. "The 'Library' of Gavin Douglas." In *Bards and Makars: Scottish Language and Literature (Medieval and Renaissance)*, ed. A. J. Aitken, Matthew P. McDiarmid, and Derik S. Thomson (Glasgow: University of Glasgow Press, 1977), pp. 107–26.

Baxter, J. W. *William Dunbar: A Biographical Study.* Edinburgh: Oliver and Boyd, 1952.

Beattie, William. "A Fragment of The Palyce of Honour." *Edinburgh Bibliographical Society Transactions* 3 (1951), 33–46.

Bisset, Habakkuk. *Habakkuk Bisset's Rolment of Courtis.* Ed. Sir Philip J. Hamilton-Grierson. 3 vols. Scottish Text Society n.s. 10, 13, 18. Edinburgh: William Blackwood and Sons, 1920–26.

Blyth, Charles. *"The Knychtlyke Stile": A Study of Gavin Douglas'* Aeneid. Cambridge: Harvard University Press, 1963. Rpt. New York and London: Garland, 1987.

Boccaccio, Giovanni. *Dizionario geografico*. [Italian translation of *De montibus, silvis, fontibus, lacubus, fluminibus, stagnis seu paludibus, et de nominibus maris*.] Trans. Nicolò Liburnio. Turin: Fògola, 1978.

———. *Forty-Six Lives Translated from Boccaccio's De Claris Mulieribus by Henry Parker, Lord Morley*. Ed. Herbert G. Wright. *EETS* 214 (1943).

The Bodley Version of Mandeville's Travels. Ed. M. C. Seymour. *EETS* 253 (1963).

Brown, Peter Hume. *Early Travellers in Scotland*. Edinburgh: Douglass, 1891.

———. *Scotland before 1700 from Contemporary Documents*. Edinburgh: Douglass, 1893.

The Buke of the Sevyne Sagis. Ed. Catherine van Buuren. Leiden: Leiden University Press, 1982.

Cairns, Sandra. *"The Palice of Honour* of Gavin Douglas, Ovid and Raffaello Regio's Commentary on Ovid's *Metamorphoses."* *Res Publica Litterarum* 7 (1984), 17–38.

Campbell, J. F. *Popular Tales of the West Highlands*. 4 vols. Paisley: Gairdner, 1890.

Carter, Henry Holland. *A Dictionary of Middle English Musical Terms*. Indiana University Humanities Series 45. Bloomington: Indiana University Press, 1961.

Chaucer, Geoffrey. *The Riverside Chaucer*. Ed. Larry D. Benson et al. Boston: Houghton Mifflin, 1987.

The Chepman and Myllar Prints. Ed. William Beattie. Oxford: Edinburgh Bibliographical Society, 1950.

The Court of Sapience. Ed. E. Ruth Harvey. Toronto: University of Toronto Press, 1984.

Curtius, Ernst Robert. *European Literature and the Latin Middle Ages*. Trans. Willard Trask. 1948. New York: Pantheon, 1953.

Doob, Penelope Reed. *The Idea of the Labyrinth from Classical Antiquity through the Middle Ages.* Ithaca, N.Y.: Cornell University Press, 1990.

[DOST] The Dictionary of the Older Scottish Tongue. Ed. W. A. Craigie, A. J. Aitken, J. Stevenson, and H. Watson. University of Chicago Press and Aberdeen University Press, 1931–. [A–Ro.]

Douglas, Gavin. *Virgil's Aeneid Translated into Scottish Verse by Gavin Douglas,* ed. David F. C. Coldwell. 4 vols. Scottish Text Society 3rd series 25, 27, 28, 30. Edinburgh and London: William Blackwood and Sons, 1957–64.

Dowden, John. *The Medieval Church in Scotland.* Glasgow: J. MacLehose and Sons, 1988.

Dunbar, William. *The Poems of William Dunbar.* Ed. James Kinsley. Oxford: Clarendon, 1979.

Ebin, Lois. *Illuminator, Makar, Vates: Visions of Poetry in the Fifteenth Century.* Lincoln: University of Nebraska Press, 1988.

The Exchequer Rolls of Scotland. Vol. 11: 1497–1501. Ed. George Burnett. Edinburgh: H. M. General Register House, 1888.

[Fordun, John of.] *Chronica gentis Scotorum. John of Fordun's Chronicle of the Scottish Nation [Scottichronicon].* Ed. W. F. Skene. Trans. F. J. H. Skene. 2 vols. Edinburgh: Edmonston and Douglas, 1871.

Fox, Denton. "The Scottish Chaucerians." In *Chaucer and Chaucerians,* ed. Derek Brewer (London: Nelson, 1966), pp. 193–200.

Fradenburg, Louise Olga. *City, Marriage, Tournament: Arts of Rule in Late Medieval Scotland.* Madison: University of Wisconsin Press, 1991.

Gower, John. *The English Works of John Gower.* Ed. G. C. Macaulay. 2 vols. *EETS* e.s. 81, 82 (1900–01). Rpt. 1957.

Haye, Gilbert of the. *Gilbert of the Haye's Prose Manuscript (1456).* Ed. J. H. Stevenson. Scottish Text Society 1st series 44, 62. Edinburgh: William Blackwood, 1901–14.

Henryson, Robert. *The Poems of Robert Henryson.* Ed. Denton Fox. Oxford: Clarendon, 1981.

Herd, David. *Ancient and Modern Scottish Songs, Heroic Ballads etc.* 2 vols. [1776] Edinburgh: Scottish Academic Press, 1973.

Holland, Richard. *The Buke of the Howlat.* In *Longer Scottish Poems Volume One: 1375–1650,* ed. Priscilla Bawcutt and Felicity Riddy (Edinburgh: Scottish Academic Press, 1987), pp. 43–84, 323–40.

Kratzmann, Gregory. *Anglo-Scottish Literary Relations 1430–1550.* Cambridge University Press, 1979.

Lewis, C. S. *The Allegory of Love.* London: Oxford University Press, 1936.

Liber Pluscardensis. Ed. W. F. Skene. Edinburgh: Blackwood, 1885.

Lindsay, Sir David. *The Works of Sir David Lindsay.* Ed. Douglas Hamer. Scottish Text Society 3rd series 1, 2, 6, 8. Edinburgh: William Blackwood, 1931–36.

Lydgate, John. *Lydgate's Fall of Princes.* Ed. Henry Bergen. 4 vols. *EETS* e.s. 121–24 (1918–19). Rpt. 1967.

——. *Lydgate's Siege of Thebes.* Ed. Axel Erdmann and Eilert Ekwall. 2 vols. *EETS* e.s. 108, 125 (1911, 1930). Rpt. 1960, 1973.

——. *Lydgate's Troy Book.* Ed. Henry Bergen. 4 vols. *EETS* e.s. 97, 103, 106, 126 (1906, 1908, 1910, 1920). Rpt. 1973–75.

——. *Poems.* Ed. John Norton-Smith. Oxford: Clarendon Press, 1966.

Marcuse, Sibyl. *A Survey of Musical Instruments.* New York: Harper, 1975.

[MED] Middle English Dictionary. Ed. Hans Kurath, Sherman M. Kuhn, J. Reidy, and Robert E. Lewis. Ann Arbor: University of Michigan Press, 1952–. [A–Stok.]

Mertes, Kate. *The English Noble Household 1250–1600.* Oxford: Blackwell, 1988.

Mill, Anna Jean. *Medieval Plays in Scotland.* Edinburgh: William Blackwood, 1927.

Morse, Ruth. "Gavin Douglas: 'Off Eloquence the flowand balmy strand.'" In *Chaucer Traditions: Studies in Honour of Derek Brewer,* ed. Ruth Morse and Barry Windeatt (Cambridge: Cambridge University Press, 1990), pp. 107–21.

Nicholson, Ranald. *Scotland: The Later Middle Ages.* Edinburgh: Oliver and Boyd, 1974.

Nitecki, Alicia K. "Gavin Douglas's Yelling Fish: *The Palice of Honour,* Lines 146–8." *Notes and Queries* 226 (1981), 118–19.

Norton-Smith, John. "Ekphrasis as a Stylistic Element in Douglas's *Palis of Honoure.*" *Medium Aevum* 48 (1979), 240–53.

[OED] *Oxford English Dictionary.* Ed. J. A. H. Murray, Henry Bradley, W. A. Craigie, and C. T. Onions, with Supplement ed. R. W. Burchfield. 2nd ed. Ed. J. A. Simpson and E. S. C. Weiner. Oxford: Clarendon Press, 1989.

On the Properties of Things: John Trevisa's Translation of Bartholomaeus Anglicus De Proprietatibus Rerum. Ed. M. C. Seymour et al. 2 vols. Oxford: Clarendon Press, 1975.

Panofsky, Erwin. *Studies in Iconology.* 2nd ed. New York: Harper and Row, 1962.

Parkinson, David. "The Farce of Modesty in Gavin Douglas's *The Palis of Honoure.*" *Philological Quarterly* 70 (1990), 13–25.

——. "Mobbing Scenes in Middle Scots Verse: Holland, Douglas, Dunbar." *Journal of English and Germanic Philology* 85 (1986), 494–509.

Pearsall, Derek. *John Lydgate.* London: Routledge and Kegan Paul; Charlottesville, Va.: University Press of Virginia, 1970.

Spearing, A. C. *Medieval Dream-Poetry.* Cambridge: Cambridge University Press, 1976.

Thorndike, Lynn. *A History of Magic and Experimental Science.* Vol. 2. New York: Macmillan, 1929.

Tristram, Philippa. *Figures of Life and Death in Medieval English Literature.* London: Paul Elek, 1976.

Utley, Francis Lee. *The Crooked Rib: An Analytical Index to the Argument about Women in English and Scots Literature to the End of the Year 1568.* Columbus: Ohio State University Press, 1944.

Whiting, Bartlett Jere, and Helen Wescott Whiting. *Proverbs, Sentences, and Proverbial Phrases from English Writings Mainly before 1500.* Cambridge, Mass.: Belknap Press, 1968.

Woolf, Rosemary. *The English Religious Lyric in the Middle Ages.* Oxford: Clarendon, 1968.

The Palis of Honoure

The Prologue

	Quhen pale Aurora with face lamentable	*When; mournful face*
	Hir russat mantill, borderit all with sable,	*reddish-brown cloak; fringed*
	Lappit about be hevinlye circumstance	*Wrapped; with divine ceremoniousness*
	The tender bed and arres honorable	*soft; tapestry*
5	Of Flora, quene till flouris amyable	*a kindly queen to the flowers*
	In May, I rays to do my observance	*arose; customary ritual*
	And entrit in a garding of plesance	*entered; an enclosed garden*
	With Sole depaint, as Paradys amyable,	*Painted by the Sun, lovely as Paradise*
	And blisfull bewes with blomed variance,	*boughs; variety of blossoms*

10	So craftely Dame Flora had overfret	*skilfully; ornamented over*
	Hir hevinly bed — powderit with mony a set	*spangled; cluster*
	Of ruby, topas, perle and emerant,	*emerald*
	With balmy dewe bathit and kyndly wet,	*suitably*
	Quhil vapours hote — right fresche and wele ybet,	*Until; amply supplied*
15	Dulce of odour, of flewour most fragrant —	*Sweet; scent*
	The silver droppis on dayseis distillant,	*drops; daisies; trickling*
	Quhilk verdour branches over the alars yet,[1]	
	With smoky sence the mystis reflectant.[2]	

	The fragrant flouris, blomand in their seis,	*blooming; dwelling-places*
20	Overspred the leves of Naturis tapestreis,	*leaves; tapestries*
	Above the quhilk, with hevinly armoneis,	*which; harmonies*
	The birdes sat on twistes and on greis,	*twigs; branches*
	Melodiously makand thair kyndely gleis,	*making their own songs*
	Quhois schill notis fordinned al the skyis.	*Whose; shrill; resounded through*
25	Of reparcust ayr, the eccon cryis	*[Because] of reverberating air; echo sounds*
	Amang the branches of the blomed treis;	*trees in blossom*
	And on the laurers, silver droppis lyis.	*laurels*

---

[1] *Which greenness (the) branches poured upon the garden paths*

[2] *Diverting the mists with [a] smoky incense*

15

	Quhyll that I rowmed in that paradice	*While; roamed*
	Replennessed and full of all delice,	*Replenished; delight*
30	Out of the sea Eous alift his heid —	*lifted*
	I meyne the hors quhilk drawis at device	*mean; which pulls with perfect skill*
	The assiltre and goldin chaire of pryce	*axletree; of great worth*
	Of Tytan, quhilk at morowe semis reid.	*(the Sun) who appears red at morning*
	The new colour that all the night lay deid	*dead*
35	Is restored. Baith fowlis, flowris, and ryce	*birds, flowers; branches*
	Reconfort was throw Phebus gudlyheid.	*Invigorated; Apollo's benevolence*
	The dasy and the maryguld onlappit	*spread open*
	Quhilkis all the nicht lay with thair levis happit	*Which; night; leaves plucked up*
	Thaim to preserve fra rewmes pungitive.	*harmful moisture; stinging*
40	The umbrate treis that Tytan about wappit	*shady trees; wrapped*
	War portrait and on the erth yschappit	*outlined*
	Be goldin bemes vivificative	*life-giving*
	Quhois amene hete is most restorative.	*pleasant heat*
	The gershoppers amangis the vergers gnappit	*among the gardens nibbled*
45	And beis wrocht materiall for thair hyve.	*bees made*
	Richt halsom was the sessoun of the yeir.	*healthful; season*
	Phebus furth yet depured bemes cleir	*poured forth; purified*
	Maist nutrityve tyll all thynges vigitant.	*nutritious for; growing*
	God Eolus of wynd list nocht appeir,	*Aeolus; chose not to appear*
50	Nor ald Saturne with his mortall speir	*old; deadly spear*
	And bad aspect, contrar til every plant.	*astrological influence*
	Neptunus nolde within that palace hant.	*did not want; to frequent*
	The beriall stremes rynnyng men micht heir	*crystal (clear, pale green)*
	By bonkis grene with glancis variant.	*gleams changeful*
55	For till beholde that hevinly place complete —	*to see; entire*
	The purgit ayr with new engendrit hete,	*cleansed; newly generated heat*
	The soyl enbroude with colowr, ure and stone,	*stained; ore; jewel*
	The tender grene, the balmy droppes swete —	*soft; fragrant*
	So rejoysit and confort wes my sprete	*comforted; spirit*
60	I not wes it a vision or fanton.[1]	

---

[1] *I did not know whether it were vision or illusion*

Amyd the buskys rowmyng myn allone — *bushes roaming by myself*
Within that garth of all plesans replete, — *enclosed garden*
A voce I hard, preclare as Phebus schone — *as brilliant as the sun shone*

Syngand, "O May thow myrrour of soles, — *paragon of comfort*
65 Maternall moneth, lady and maistres, — *month*
Tyl every thing adoun respirature, — *down (here) revive*
Thyn hevinly werk and worthy craftines — *valuable skill*
The small herbis constrenis tyl encres. — *compels to thrive*
O verray ground tyl werking of nature — *true foundation; operation*
70 Quhois hie curage and assucuryt cure — *Whose high vigour; constant care*
Causis the erth his frutis tyll expres, — *produce*
Dyffundant grace on every creature. — *Pouring forth*

"Thy godly lore, cunnyng incomparabyl, — *goodly; incomparable skill*
Dantis the savage bestis maist unstabyl — *Subdues; beasts; changeable*
75 And expellis all that nature infestis. —
The knoppit syonys with levys agreabyl — *budding shoots; pleasant*
For tyl revert and burgione ar maid abyll. — *recover; sprout; capable*
Thy myrth refreschis birdis in thair nestis, —
Quhilkis the to pryse and Nature never restis, — *praise*
80 Confessand you maist potent and lovabyll — *powerful*
Amang the brownys of the olyve twystes. — *twigs; olive branches*

"In the is rute and augment of curage. — *thee; root and increase; vigour*
In the enforcis Martis vassalage. — *thee intensifies; service to Mars*
In the is amorus luf and armony — *love; harmony*
85 With incrementis fresche in lusty age. — *increases; age of youth*
Quha that constrenit ar in luffis rage — *Whoever; confined; love's passion*
Addressand thaim with observans ayrly[1] —
Weil auchtyst the tyl glore and magnify." — *ought to glorify and praise thee*
And with that word I rasyt my vissage — *raised my face*
90 Sore effrayit, half in a frenisye. — *afraid; frenzy*

"O Nature Queen and O ye lusty May," —
Quod I tho, "Quhow lang sall I thus forvay, — *then; How long shall; stray*

---

[1] *Preparing themselves with early morning worship*

	Quhilk yow and Venus in this garth deservis?	*Who; enclosed garden serves*
	Reconsell me out of this gret affray	*Recover me; great alarm*
95	That I maye synge yow laudis day be day.	*early morning worship*
	Ye that al mundane creaturis preservis	*earthly*
	Confort your man that in this fanton stervis	*apparition suffers*
	With sprete arrasyt and every wit away,	*spirit uprooted*
	Quakyng for fere, baith puncys, vane and nervis."	*Trembling; fear; pulse; veins*

100	My fatall werd, my febyl wit I wary,	*allotted destiny; curse*
	My dasyt heid, quham lake of brane gart vary[1]	
	And not sustene so amyabyll a soun!	*endure; such a lovely sound*
	With ery curage, febyl strenthis sary,	*timid; miserable*
	Bownand me hame and list no langer tary,[2]	
105	Out of the ayr come ane impressioun	*a meteoric flash*
	Throw quhois lycht in extasy or swoun,	*whose; rapture or swoon*
	Amyd the virgultis all in tyl a fary	*thickets; altogether in a daze*
	As femynine so feblyt fell I doun.	*As enfeebled as a woman*

	And with that gleme so dasyt wes my mycht	*brilliant light; benumbed; strength*
110	Quhill thair remanit nothir voce nor sycht,	*Until; neither*
	Breth, motione, nor hetis naturale.	*natural warmth*
	Saw nevir man so faynt a levand wycht,	*living person*
	And na ferly, for over-excelland lycht	*no wonder*
	Corruppis the wit and garrys the blud availe	*Spoils; causes; descend*
115	On tyl the hart that it no danger ale —	*Unto; so that no danger harm it*
	Quhen it is smorit, membris wyrkes not richt:	*smothered; limbs*
	The dredfull terrour sua did me assaile.	*thus*

	Yyt at the last (I not quhou long a space)	*how*
	A lytell hete aperyt in my face	*appeared*
120	Quhilk had tofore beyn pale and voyde of blud.	*Which; before; empty of blood*
	Tho in my sweven I met a ferly cace:	*dream; strange occurrence*
	I thought me set within a desert place	*uninhabited*
	Amyd a forest by a hydous flud	*a hideous river*
	With grysly fysche, and shortly tyl conclud	*terrifying fish*

---

[1] *My dazed head, which lack of brain caused to wander*

[2] *Preparing myself to go and not wishing to tarry longer*

125	I shall descryve (as God wil geve me grace)	
	Myn avision in rurell termes rude.	*monitory dream; rough rustic words*

The First Part

	Thow barrant wyt overset with fantasyis,	*barren; overcome by illusions*
	Schaw now the craft that in thy memor lyis,	*Show; memory*
	Schaw now thy shame, schaw now thy bad nystee,	*wicked folly*
130	Schaw thyn endyt, repruf of rethoryis,	*writing; scorn; rhetoricians*
	Schaw now thy beggit termis mare than thryis,	*thrice-begged terms*
	Schaw now thy ranys and thyn harlottree,	*doggerel; ribaldry*
	Schaw now thy dull exhaust inanytee,	*worn-out inanity*
	Schaw furth thy cure and wryte their frenesyis	*duty; these frenzies*
135	Quhilkis of thy sempyll cunnyng nakyt the.	*humble ability stripped you*

	My ravyst sprete in that deserte terrybill	*entranced spirit*
	Approchit nere that ugly flude horrybill,	*Came near; river*
	Lyk tyll Cochyte the ryver infernall,	*Cocytus*
	Wyth vyle wattyr quhilk maid a hydduus trubbyll	*which; disturbance*
140	Rynnand overhed, blud red, and — impossybyll	*Flowing headlong*
	That it had byn a ryver naturall —	
	With brayis bare, raif rochis lyke to fall,	*steep banks; overhanging*
	Quhareon na gers nor herbys wer visibyll,	*Upon which; grass*
	Bot skauppis brynt with blastis boryall.[1]	

145	Thys laythly flude rumland as thondyr routyt	*loathly; rumbling; roared*
	In quham the fysche yelland as elvys schoutyt.	*which; yelling like elves*
	Thair yelpis wylde my hering all fordevyt.	*deafened*
	Tha grym monsturis my spretis abhorryt and doutyt.	*Those; loathed and dreaded*
	Not throu the soyl bot muskan treis sproutyt	*Nothing; rotten trees*
150	Combust, barrant, unblomyt and unlevyt,[2]	
	Ald rottyn runtis quhairin no sap was levyt	*Old rotten stump; left*
	Moch, all wast, widdrit, with granis moutyt:	*Decayed; withered; seeds fallen off*
	A ganand den quhair morthurars men revyt.	*fitting; murderers; robbed*

---

[1] *But instead, rocky knolls parched by northern winds*

[2] *Burnt, barren, without blossoms or leaves*

Quhairfore my selvyn was richt sore agast.   *I myself; very sorely afraid*

155 This wyldernes abhomynable and wast

In quhome na thing wes Nature confortand[1]

Was dyrk as royk the quhilk the see upcast.   *dark; fog; sea had cast up*

The quhislyng wynd blew mony byttir blast,   *whistling*

Runtis ratlit and uneth myght I stand: *Tree-stumps; hardly*

160 Out throu the wode I crap on fut and hand.   *through; crept*

The ryvar stank, the treis clattryt fast,

The soil was not bot marres, slyik, and sand.   *nothing but; marsh; mud*

And not but caus my spretis were abaysit   *not without cause; confounded*

All solitare in that desert arrasyt.   *snatched away*

165 "Allas," I said, "is non other remede?   *is there no other way out*

Cruel Fortoun, quhy hes thow me betrasyt?   *why have you betrayed me*

Quhy hes thow thus my fatall end compasyt?   *fated end; plotted*

Allas, allas, sall I thus sone be dede   *shall; soon*

In this desert, and wait non uther rede,   *expect no other remedy*

170 Bot be devoryt wyth sum best ravanus?   *Than to be devoured by; beast*

I wepe, I wale, I plene, I cry, I plede: *wail; lament; plead*

Inconstant warld and quheil contrarius!   *perverse wheel*

"Thy transitory plesans quhat avaylys?   *What use are your fleeting pleasures?*

Now thare, now heir, now hie and now devalys;   *[it] sinks*

175 Now to, now fro, now law, now magnifyis;   *low; becomes greater*

Now hote, now cald, now lauchys, now bewalys;   *laughs; laments*

Now seik, now hail, now wery, now not alys;   *sick; healthy; nothing is wrong*

Now gud, now evyll, now wetis, and now dryis;   *now gets wet, and now, dry*

Now thow promittis and rycht now thou denyis;   *promises*

180 Now wo, now weill, now ferm, now frevilus,   *steadfast; fickle*

Now gam, now gram, now lovys, now defyis: *mirth; anger; flatters; despises*

Inconstant warld and quheil contrarius!   *wheel*

"Ha! quha suld haif affyans in thy blys?   *confidence*

Ha! quha suld haif fyrm esperans in this   *firm hope*

185 Quhilk is, allace, sa freuch and variant?   *frail and inconstant*

Certis none. Sum hes! No wicht. Suythly, yis!   *Certainly; Truly yes*

---

[1] *In which Nature sustained no (living) thing*

Than hes my self bene gylty? Ya iwys.   *Yes indeed*
Thairfore, allace, sall danger thus me dant?   *subdue*
Quhyddyr is bycum sa sone this duyly hant   *gloomy spot*
190   And Veyr translat in wyntyr furyus?   *Spring turned into*
Thus I bewale my faitis repugnant: *fate*
Inconstant warld and quheil contrarius!"

Bydand the deid thus in myn extasy,   *Awaiting death; stupor*
A dyn I hard approchyng fast me be   *noise; close by me*
195   Quhilk movit fra the plage septentrionall   *Which; from the north side*
As heyrd of bestis stampyng with loud cry.   *Like a herd of beasts*
Bot than God wate how afferyt wes I   *God knows; afraid*
Traistand tyl be stranglyt with bestiall.   *Expecting to be killed by cattle*
Amyd a stok richt prevaly I stall   *I withdrew inside a hollow tree very stealthily*
200   Quhare lukand out anone I dyd espy   *Where, looking out, I suddenly saw*
Ane lusty rout of bestis rationall —   *A fine crowd of reasoning beasts*

Of ladyis fair and gudly men arrayit   *dressed*
In constant weid — that weil my spretis payit.   *uniform clothing; gratified my spirits*
Wyth degest mynd quhairin all wyt aboundyt   *tranquil; wherein*
205   Full sobyrly thair haknais thay assait   *saddle-horses; "put through their paces"*
Eftyr the feitis auld, and not forvayt.[1]
Thair hie prudence schew furth, and nothyng roundit,[2]
With gude effere, quhare at the wod resoundyt.[3]
In stedfast ordour, to vysy onaffrayit   *unafraid to look about*
210   Thay rydyng furth with stabylnes ygroundyt.   *trained with thoroughness*

Amyddys quham, borne in ane goldyn chare   *Amidst whom; a golden chariot*
Ovyrfret with perle and stonys maist preclare   *Covered over; gems; brilliant*
That drawin wes by haiknays four, mylk quhyt,   *pulled; four horses, milk-white*
Was set a quene, as lylly swete of sware,   *lily fair; neck*
215   In purpur robe hemmid with gold ilk gare   *each gore (wedge-shaped cloth)*
Quhilk jemmyt claspes closyd all parfyte,   *gemmed clasps*
A diademe maist pleasandly polyte   *polished*

---

[1] *According to traditional practices, and did not go astray*

[2] *They expressed their high wisdom, and did not whisper at all*

[3] *In a suitable manner, at which the forest echoed*

Set on the tressys of her gyltyn hare   *her golden hair*
And in her hand a sceptre of delyte.

220   Syne next her, rayed in granyt violate,[1]
    Twelve damysylles, ilk ane in theyr estate   *damsels, each one in her own rank*
    Quhilkis semyt of hyr consell most secre[2]
    And nixt thaym wes a lusty rout, God wate —   *fine company; knows*
    Lordis, ladyis, and mony fair prelate,   *church dignitary*
225   Baith borne of hie estate and law degre,   *high rank and low degree*
    Furth with thair quene thay al by-passit me.   *went past*
    Ane esy pase thay rydyng furth the gate   *Unhurriedly they rode on their way*
    And I abaid alone within the tre.   *I remained*

    And as the rout wes passyt one and one   *company*
230   And I remanand in the tre alone,   *remaining*
    Out throw the wode come rydand cativis twane,   *came riding two wretches*
    Ane on ane asse, a wedy about his mone,   *One; donkey; rope; mane*
    The tothir raid ane hiddows hors apone.   *other; rode*
    I passyt furth and fast at thaym did frane   *came out; eagerly asked them*
235   Quhat men thay wer. Thay answeryt me agane,
    "Our namys ben Achitefel and Synone   *Ahithophel*
    That by our suttell menys feil hes slane."   *cunning means murdered many*

    "Wait ye," quod I, "quhat signifyis yon rout?"   *Do you know*
    Synon sayd "Ya!" — and gave ane hyddows schout —   *shout*
240   "We wrechys bene abject thairfra, iwys.   *cast out from thence, indeed*
    Yone is the Quene of Sapience, but dout,   *without*
    Lady Minerve, and yone twelve hir about
    Ar the prudent Sibillais ful of blys,   *Sibyls*
    Cassandra, eik Delbora and Circis,   *also Deborah; Circe*
245   The fatale systeris twynand our weirdes out,   *spinning out our destinies*
    Judith, Jael, and mony a prophetis   *prophetess*

    "Quhilkis groundyt ar in fyrm intelligens.   *secure understanding*
    And thair is als in to yone court gone hens   *also; hence*

---

[1] *Then after her, dressed in grain-dyed violet clothes,*

[2] *Who seemed discreet members of her council*

	Clerkis divine with problewmys curius	*puzzling questions*
250	As Salomon the well of sapiens	*the source of wisdom*
	And Arestotyl, fulfyllet of prudens,	*Aristotle, well-stocked with wisdom*
	Salust, Senek and Titus Livius,	*Seneca; Livy*
	Picthagoras, Porphure, Permenydus,	*Pythagoras, Porphyry, Parmenides*
	Melysses with his sawis but defence,	*Melissus; incontrovertible sayings*
255	Sidrag, Secundus and Solenyus,	*Shadrach; Solinus*

	"Ptholomeus, Ipocras, Socrates,	*Ptolemy, Hippocrates*
	Empedocles, Neptennebus, Hermes,	*Nectanabus, Hermes Trismegistus*
	Galien, Averroes and Plato,	
	Enoth, Lameth, Job and Diogenes,	*Enoch, Lamech*
260	The eloquent and prudent Ulisses,	
	Wyse Josephus and facund Cicero,	*eloquent*
	Melchisedech, with othyr mony mo.	*Melchizedek*
	Thair viage lyis throw out this wildernes.	*Their route passes through*
	To the Palice of Honour all thay go,	

265	Is situat from hens liggis ten hundyr.	*a thousand leagues hence*
	Our horsys oft or we be thair wyll fundyr.	*before we get there; go lame*
	Adew, we may no langer heir remane."	
	"Or that ye passe," quod I, "tell me this wondyr,	*Before you go*
	How that ye wrechyt cativis thus at undyr	*in this low position*
270	Ar sociat with this court soverane?"	*associated*
	Achitefell maid this answer agane:	
	"Knawis thou not? Haill, erd-quake, and thundyr	*earthquake*
	Ar oft in May, with mony schour of rane.	*shower; rain*

	"Rycht so we bene in tyll this company.	
275	Our wyt aboundit, and usyt wes lewdly.	*wickedly*
	My wysdome ay fulfyllyt my desyre	*always*
	As thou may in the Bybyl weil aspy,	*well see*
	How Davidis prayer put my counsell by.	*caused my advice to be set aside*
	I gart his sonne aganys hym conspyre,	*I made*
280	The quhilk wes slane. Quhairfore up be the swyre	*For that reason; neck*
	My self I hangit, frustrat sa fowlily.	*in so humiliating a way*
	This Synon wes a Greik that rasyt fyre	*started*

First in to Troy, as Virgyll dois report.

23

	Sa tratourlyk maid him be draw overwhort	*by an unfortunate draw of lots*
285	Quhill in he brocht the Hors with men of armys	
	Quhairthrow the towne distroit wes at schort."	*By which means; destroyed*
	Quod I, "Is this your destany and sort?	*destiny and fate*
	Cursit be he that sorowis for your harmys,	*grieves for your injuries*
	For ye bene schrewis baith, be Goddis armys!	*malicious men both*
290	Ye will optene nane entres at yone port	*gain no entry at that gate*
	Bot gif it be throw sorcery or charmys."	*Unless it be through*

	"Ingres tyll have," quod thay, "we not presume.	*Entry*
	It sufficis us tyl se the Palice blume	*flourish*
	And stand on rowme quhare bettyr folk bene charrit.[1]	
295	For tyll remane, adew, we have na tume.	*no time*
	This ilk way cummis the courtis, be our dume,	*very way; by our estimation*
	Of Diane and Venus that feil hes marryt."	*who has troubled many*
	With that thay raid away as thay war skarryt,	*rode; as if they were scared*
	And I agayne, maist lyk ane elrych grume,	*elvish fellow*
300	Crap in the muskane akyn stok mysharrit.	*Crept; rotten oak-stumps; decrepit*

	Thus wrechitly I maid my resydence	
	Imagynand feil syse for sum defence	*many means*
	In contrar savage bestis maist cruell,	*Against*
	For na remeid bot deid be violence,	*no remedy except death*
305	Sum tyme, asswagis febill indegence.	*alleviates; destitution*
	Thus in a part I reconfort my sell	*somewhat; console*
	Bot that so lityll wes I dar nocht tell.	
	The stychlyng of a mows out of presence	*squeaking of a mouse*
	Had bene to me mare ugsum than the Hell.	*horrible*

310	Yit glaid I wes that I with thaym had spokkyn.	*glad*
	Had not bene that, certis my hart had brokkyn	*certainly*
	For megirnes and pusillamytee.	*weakness and timidity*
	Remanand thus within the tre al lokkyn,	*Staying; enclosed*
	Dissyrand fast sum signys or sum tokkyn	*Desiring; token*
315	Of Lady Venus and of hir companee,	
	A hart transformyt ran fast by the tree	

---

[1] *And stand at a distance, where better folk are turned away*

With houndis rent, on quham Dian wes wrokkyn. *whom; avenged*
Tharby I understude that sche wes nee. *nigh*

Thay had tofore declarit hir cummyng:
320   Mare perfytly forthy I knew the syng. *therefore; sign*
Wes Action quhilk Diane nakyt watyt *who spied on Diana when she was naked*
Bathyng in a well and eik hir madynnys yyng. *and also; young maidens*
The goddes wes commovyt at this thing *angered*
And hym in forme hes of a hart translatit. *transformed*
325   I saw, allace, his houndis at him slatit. *his dogs set on him*
Bakwert he blent to gyf thaym knawlegyng *glanced; give them*
Tha raif thair lord, mysknew hym at thaym batit.[1]

Syne ladyis come with lusty giltyn tressys, *Then; golden hair*
In habit wild maist lyke till fostaressys, *outdoor clothing; women foresters*
330   Amyddys quham heich on ane eliphant *Amidst whom high*
In syng that sche in chastite incressys *As a sign that she grows in chastity*
Raid Diane that ladyis hartis dressys *Rode; prepares*
Tyl be stabil and na way inconstant.
God wait that nane of thaym is variant: *knows; none of them is fickle*
335   All chast and trew virginite professys. *acknowledge*
I not, bot few I saw with Diane hant. *do not know; associate*

Intil that court I saw anone present *In; soon*
Jeptyis douchtir, a lusty lady gent *Jephthah's; noble*
Offeryt tyl God in hir virginite.
340   Pollixena, I wys, wes not absent;
Panthessile with mannys hardyment, *Penthesileia; manly fortitude*
Effygyn and Virgenius' douchter fre, *Iphigenia*
With uthyr flouris of feminyte, *other*
Baith of the New and the Ald Testament,
345   All on thay raid and left me in the tre.

In that desert dispers in sondyr skattryt *scattered about*
Wer bewis bare quham rane and wynde on battryt. *bare branches; battered*
The water stank, the feild was odious

---

[1] *But they ripped their lord apart — did not recognize him who fed them*

Quhar dragonys, lessertis, askis, edders swattryt   *lizards, asps, adders wallowed*

350   With mouthis gapand, forkyt tayles tattryt,   *gaping; tattered*

With mony a stang and spoutis vennomous   *sting; poisonous squirts*

Corruppyng ayr be rewme contagious.   *Corrupting the air with noxious moisture*

Maist gros and vyle enposonyt clowdis clatteryt,[1]

Rekand lyk hellys smoke sulfuryus.   *Reeking*

355   My dasyt hed fordullit dissyly   *dazed head stupefied dizzily*

I rasyt up, half in a letergy,   *raised; lethargy*

As dois a catyve ydronken in slep   *wretch overcome by sleep*

And so opperyt tyl my fantasy   *appeared to my powers of perception*

A schynand lycht out of the northest sky.   *shining light*

360   Proportion sounding dulcest hard I pepe   *sweetest-sounding measure I heard "peep"*

The quhilk with cure till heir I did tak kepe.[2]

In musyk nowmer full of harmony   *numbered*

Distant on far wes caryit be the depe.   *carried by the deep [water]*

Farther by wattyr folk may soundis here   *hear*

365   Than by the erth, the quhilk with poris sere   *the which with many pores*

Up drynkis ayr that movit is by sound

Quhilk in compact wattir of ane rivere

May nocht entre bot rynnys thare and here   *enter; runs*

Quhil it at last be caryit on the ground;   *Until; unto*

370   And thocht throw dyn, be experience is found,   *although because of noise*

The fysch ar causyt within the rivere stere,   *to move*

Inoth the wattyr the nois dois not abound.   *Within*

Violent dyn the ayr brekkis and deris,   *breaks and troubles*

Syne gret motion of ayr the watyr steris.   *Then; agitates*

375   The wattyr steryt, fischis for ferdnes fleis.   *fear hasten away*

Bot, out of dout, no fysch in wattyr heris   *doubtless; hears*

For, as we se, rycht few of thaym has eris;   *very few; ears*

And eik, forsuyth, bot gyf wyse clerkis leis,   *indeed, unless wise clerks lie*

Thair is nane ayr inoth watters nor seis,   *within; seas*

380   But quhilk na thing may heir, as wyse men leiris,   *Without which; teach*

---

[1] *Most dense and filthy contaminated clouds rattled past*

[2] *The which I took care to hear with attentiveness*

Lyik as but lycht thair is na thyng that seis.   *Just as without; sees*

Anewch of this, I not quhat it may mene.   *Enough; I do not know what*
I wyll returne till declare all bedene   *all in one place together*
My dreidfull dreme with grysly fantasyis.   *terrifying*
385   I schew tofore quhat I had hard and sene,   *showed before what; heard*
Perticularly sum of my paynfull tene.   *hurtfull trouble*
But now God wate quhat ferdnes on me lyis!   *God knows what fearfulness*
Lang ere I said — and now this tyme is twyis —   *A while before; twice*
A sound I hard, of angellys as it had bene,   *heard*
390   With armony fordynnand all the skyis[1]

So dulce, so swete and so melodius   *pleasing*
That every wycht thair with mycht be joyous   *person*
Bot I and cativis dullit in dispare.   *Except*
For quhen a man is wreth or furius,   *when; angry*
395   Malancolyk for wo or tedius,   *Melancholy; bored*
Than is al plesance till hym maist contrare   *most contrary to him*
And semblably than so did wyth me fare: *similarly then*
This melody intonyt hevinly thus   *sung*
For profund wo constrenyt me mak care.   *constrained me to make lamentation*

400   And murnand thus as ane maist wofull wicht,   *mourning*
Of the maist plesand court I had a sycht   *most pleasant court; sight*
In warld adoun sen Adam wes create.[2]
Quhat sang? quhat joy? quhat armony? quhat lycht?   *What song*
Quhat myrthfull solace, plesance all at ryght?   *in good order*
405   Quhat fresch bewte? quhat excelland estate?   *display*
Quhat swete vocis? quhat wordis suggurate?   *honeyed*
Quhat fair debatis? quhat lufsum ladyis bricht?   *discussions; loveable*
Quhat lusty gallandis did on thair servyce wate?   *gentlemen; wait*

Quhat gudly pastance and quhat menstraly?   *recreation; minstrelsy*
410   Quhat game thay maid? In faith, not tell can I.   *amusement*
Thocht I had profund wit angelicall   *Even if*

---

[1] *Resounding harmoniously across the entire sky*
[2] *In the world here below since Adam was created*

The hevinly soundis of thair armony
Has dymmyt so my drery fantasy,   *dimmed; doleful delusion*
Baith wit and reason, half is lost of all.
415 Yit as I knaw, als lychtly say I sall: *so shall I readily say*
That angellyk and godly company   *goodly*
Tyll se me thocht a thyng celestiall.

Procedand furth wes draw ane chariote
Be cursuris twelf trappit in gren velvote.   *twelve war-horses adorned*
420 Of fyne gold wer juncturis and harnasyngis.   *mountings; harness*
The lymnuris wer of byrnyst gold, God wate.   *cart shafts*
Baith extre and quhelis of gold, I hote.   *axle-tree; wheels; assure (you)*
Of goldyn cord wer lyamys, and the stryngis   *reins; traces*
Festnyt conjunct in massy goldyn ryngis.   *Fastened together; solid*
425 Evyr hamys convenient for sic note   *Ivory yokes*
And raw silk brechamys ovyr thair halsys hyngis.   *horse-collars; necks*

The body of the cart of evir bone   *ivory*
With crysolytis and mony pretious stone   *chrysolites*
Wes all overfret in dew proportioun   *ornamented evenly*
430 Lyke sternys in the firmament quhilkis schone.   *stars*
Reperalit wes that godlyk plesand wone,   *Arrayed; pleasant dwelling fit for a god*
Tyldyt abone and to the erth adoun   *Curtained above*
In rychest claith of gold of purpur broun,   *cloth; dark purple*
But fas or othyr frenyeis had it none   *tassels; fringes*
435 Save plate of gold anamallyt all fassioun   *enamelled in all kinds of patterns*

Quhairfra dependant hang thair megyr bellys —   *these slender bells*
Sum round, sum thraw — in sound the quhilkis excellis.   *twisted*
All wer of gold of Araby maist fyne
Quhilkis with the wynd concordandly so knellys   *rings so harmoniously*
440 That to be glad thair sound al wycht compellys.   *everyone*
The armony wes so melodius fyne
In mannys voce and instrument divine,
Quhare so thay went, it semyt nothyng ellys   *That wherever*
Bot jerarchyes of angellys, ordours nyne.   *hierarchies*

445 Amyd the chare fulfillyt of plesance,   *abounding with delight*
A lady sat, at quhais obeysance   *at whose command*

28

Wes all that rout; and wondyr is till here	*company; to hear*
Of hir excelland lusty countenance.	
Hir hie bewte, quhilk mayst is til avance,	*which is most to be praised*
450 Precellys all — thair may be na compere —	*Surpasses; equal*
For lyk Phebus in hiest of his spere	*at the zenith of his sphere*
Hir bewtye schane, castand so gret a glance	*shone; casting; gleam of light*
All farehed it opprest, baith far and nere.	*beauty; overwhelmed, both*
Scho wes peirles of schap and portrature.	*matchless of figure and features*
455 In her had Nature fynesyt hir cure.	*perfected her jurisdiction*
As for gud havyngis, thair wes nane bot sche;	*good manners*
And hir array wes so fyne and so pure	
That quhair of wes hir rob I am not sure	*gown*
For nocht bot perle and stonys mycht I se	*nothing*
460 Of quham the brychtnes of hir hie bewtie	*which*
For till behald my sycht mycht not endure	
Mair than the brycht sonne may the bakkis e.	*the eye of a bat*
Hir hair as gold or topasis wes hewyt.	*topazes; tinged*
Quha hir beheld, hir bewtie ay renewit.	*Whoever; was revived by her beauty*
465 On heid sche had a crest of dyamantis.	
Thair wes na wycht that gat a sycht eschewyt,	*no one escaped who got a glimpse*
Wer he nevir sa constant nor weil thewyt,	*well trained*
Na he was woundit and him hir servant grantis.	*But; acknowledges*
That hevinly wycht hir cristall eyn so dantis[1]	
470 For blenkis swete nane passit unpersewyt	*glances; unassailed*
Bot gyf he wer preservit as thir sanctis.	*Unless; saints*
I wondryt sore and in mynd did stare	*was amazed*
Quhat creature that mycht be wes so fare,	*What being this might be that*
Of sa peirles excelent womanheid.	*so matchless; femininity*
475 And, farlyand thus, I saw within the chare	*wondering*
Quhare that a man wes set with lymmes square,	*sturdy limbs*
His body weil entalyeit every steid:	*well sculpted; part*
He bare a bow with dartis haw as leid;	*blue-gray; lead*
His clethyng wes als grene as ane hountare	*hunter*

---

[1] *The crystal eyes of that divine person so vanquish*

480	Bot he forsuyth had none eyn in his hed.	*truly; no eyes*
	I understude by signis persavabill	*visible signs*
	That wes Cupyd the god maist dissavabill,	*deceitful*
	The lady, Venus, his mother, a goddes.	
	I knew that wes the court so variabill	*changeable*
485	Of erdly luf quhilk sendill standis stabill.	*earthly love; seldom*
	Bot yit thair myrth and solace nevertheles	
	In musik, tone, and menstraly expres,	*pitch and performance clearly rendered*
	So craftely with corage aggreabill —	*skilfully in a fitting spirit*
	Hard never wicht sik melody, I ges.	*Heard; such; suppose*
490	Acumpanyit lusty yonkers with all.	*youths; with the rest*
	Fresche ladyis sang in voce virgineall	*maidenly voices*
	Concordes swete, divers entoned reportis.	*Harmonies; sung responses*
	Proportionis fyne with sound celestiall —	*Intervals*
	Duplat, triplat diatesseriall,	*Double and triple rhythms in fourths*
495	Sesque altra and decupla resortis,	*Fifths; repeats (see note)*
	Diapason of mony syndry sortis —	*Octaves*
	War songin and plait be seir cunnyng menstrall	*sung and played; various*
	On luf ballattis with mony fair disportis.	*balades; diversions*
	In modulation hard I play and syng	*musical proportion; heard*
500	Faburdoun, priksang, discant, conturyng,	
	Cant organe, figuration, and gemmell.[1]	
	On croud, lute, harp, with mony gudly spring.	*fiddle; fine lively dance*
	Schalmis, clarionis, portativis hard I ring,	*Reed-instruments, trumpets, organs*
	Monycord, orgain, tympane, and symbell,	*Keyboard; drum*
505	Sytholl, psalttry, and vocis swete as bell,	*Citole (guitar); hand harp*
	Soft releschyngis in dulce delyveryng,	*singing; clear enunciation*
	Fractyonis divide at rest or clos compell.	*(see note)*
	Not Pan of Archaid so plesandly plays,	*Arcadia*
	Nor King David, quhais playng, as men sayis,	*whose*
510	Conjurit the spreit the quhilk Kyng Saul confoundit,	*spirit; tormented*

---

[1] *500-01: Extemporized part-singing, notated song, melodic accompaniment, singing a third part, Simple polyphony, polyphonic variation, and two-part harmony*

	Nor Amphion with mony subtile layis	*intricate songs*
	Quhilk Thebes wallit with harpyng in his dayis,	*Who; fortified*
	Nor he that first the subtile craftis foundit	*abstruse arts*
	Was not in musik half so weil igroundit	*well-instructed*
515	Nor knew thair mesure tent dele be no wayes.	*a tenth part of what they knew*
	At thair resort baith hevyn and erd resoundit.	*coming together*

	Na mare I understude thir noumeris fyne	*intricate harmonic proportions*
	Be God than dois a gekgo or a swyne,	*cuckoo or a pig*
	Save that me think swete soundis gude to heir.	
520	Na mair heiron my labour will I tyne.	*will I waste my effort*
	Na mair I wyl thir verbillys swete diffyne,	*singing; set terms to*
	How that thair musik tones war mair cleir	*notes of music*
	And dulcer than the movyng of the speir	*sweeter; sphere*
	Or Orpheus' harp of Trace with sound divyne.	
525	Glaskeryane maid na noyes compeir.	*no sound equal (to them)*

	Thay condescend sa weil in ane accord	*concur; one*
	That by na juynt thair soundis bene discord,	*no point of contact*
	In every key thay werren sa expert.	*they were*
	Of thair array gyf I suld mak record —	
530	Lusty spryngaldis and mony gudly lord,	*young men*
	Tendyr yonglyngis with pietuous virgin hart,	*children*
	Eldar ladyis knew mair of lustis art,	*[who] knew*
	Divers utheris quhilkis me not list remord,	*whom I do not wish to recall*
	Quhais lakkest weid was silkis of brounvert —	*poorest clothing; dark green*

535	In vesturis quent of mony syndry gyse	*fine clothing; many different fashions*
	I saw all claith of gold men mycht devise,	*design*
	Purpur coulour, punyk and skarlot hewis,	*purple; reddish-yellow*
	Velvot robbis maid with the grand assyse,	*in the highest fashion*
	Dames, satyn, begaryit mony wyse,	*Damask; variegated in colour*
540	Cramessy satin, velvot enbroude in divers rewis,	*Crimson; velvet dyed; stripes*
	Satyn figuris champit with flouris and bewis,	*embroidered; branches*
	Damesflure, tere pyle quhare on thair lyis	*Flowered damask, Spanish velvet*
	Perle orphany, quhilk every state renewis.	*Gold embroidery; dignity restores*

| | Thare ryche entire, maist peirles to behald, | *Their; attire; peerless* |
| 545 | My wyt can not discrive, howbeit I wald. | *however much I would like to* |

31

	Mony entrappit stede with sylkis sere,	*caparisoned; various silks*
	Mony pattrell nervyt with gold I tald,	*horse's breastplate; banded*
	Full mony new gylt harnasyng not ald,	*trappings*
	On mony palfray lusum ladyis clere.	*saddle-horse; lovely; fair*
550	And nyxt the chare I saw formest appere,	*in front*
	Upon a bardyt cursere stout and bald,	*armored war-horse; spirited*
	Mars god of stryf enarmyt in byrnist gere:	*polished armour*

	Every invasybill wapyn on hym he bare;	*offensive weapon*
	His luke was grym, his body large and square,	
555	His lymmys weil entailyeit til be strang;	*sculpted*
	His nek wes gret, a span lenth weil or mare,	*a hand's breadth long*
	His vissage braid with crisp broun curland hare;	*curly*
	Of statur, not ovyr gret nor yit ovyr lang.	*not too large nor yet too tall*
	Behaldand Venus, "O ye my luif," he sang,	*Watching; love*
560	And scho agane with dalyans sa fare	*flirtation*
	Hir knycht hym clepis quhare so he ryde or gang.	*calls wherever; walk*

	Thair wes Arsyte and Palemon alswa	*Arcite*
	Accumpanyit with fare Emylya,	*Emily*
	The quene Dido with hir fals luf Enee,	*faithless lover Aeneas*
565	Trew Troylus, unfaythfull Cressida,	
	The fair Paris and plesand Helena,	*pleasing*
	Constant Lucres and traist Penolype,	*Faithful Lucrece; trustworthy*
	Kynd Pirramus and wobegone Thysbe,	*Loving Pyramus*
	Dolorus Progne, triest Philomena,	*Procne; sad*
570	King David's luif thare saw I, Barsabe.	*Bathsheba*

	Thare wes Ceix with the kynd Alcyon,	*loving*
	And Achilles, wroth with Agamemnon	*angry*
	For Bryssida his lady fra hym tane,	*Briseis; from; taken*
	Wofull Phillys with hir luf Demoophan,	*Phyllis; Demophoon*
575	Subtel Medea and hir knycht Jasone.	*Artful*
	Of France I saw thair Paris and Veane.	*Vienne*
	Thare wes Phedra, Thesyus and Adriane,	*Ariadne*
	The secrete wyse hardy Ipomedon,	*brave*
	Asswere, Hester, irraprevabill Susane.	*Ahasuerus, Esther, blameless Susanna*

| 580 | Thare wes the fals unhappy Dalida, | *unfortunate Delilah* |

	Cruel wikkyt and curst Dyonera,	*Deianeira*
	Wareit Bibles and the fair Absolon,	*Accursed Byblis*
	Ysyphele, abhomynabil Sylla,	*Scylla*
	Trastram, Yside, Helcana and Anna,	*Tristram, Iseult, Elkanah; Hannah*
585	Cleopatra and worthy Mark Anthon,	
	Iole, Hercules, Alcest, Ixion,	
	The onely pacient wyfe Gressillida,	*Griselde*
	Nersissus, that his hed brak on a ston.	*Narcissus, who broke his head*

	Thare wes Jacob with fair Rachel his make,	*wife*
590	The quhilk become til Laban for hir sake	*Who*
	Fourteen yere boynd with fyrm hart immutabill —	*contracted; unchangeable*
	Thair bene bot few sic now, I undertake:	*There are only a few such*
	Thir fair ladyis in silk and claith of lake	*These; cloth of fine linen*
	Thus lang sall not all foundyn be so stabyll.	*For this long; dependable*
595	This Venus court quhilk wes in luif maist abil	*most adept*
	For till discrive my cunning is to wake.	*describe my skill is too weak*
	A multitude thay wer, innumerabill,	

	Of gudly folk in every kynd and age.	
	With blenkis swete, fresch lusty grene curage,	*glances; flourishing vigour*
600	And dalians thay rydyng furth in fere.	*flirtation; ride on together*
	Sum leivys in hope and sum in great thyrlage,	*Some live; servitude*
	Sum in dispare, sum findis his panys swage.	*pains decrease*
	Garlandis of flouris and rois chaplettis sere	*various wreaths of roses*
	Thay bare on hede and samyn sang so clere	*wore; together*
605	Quhil that thair myrth commovit my curage	*Until; stirred my spirits*
	Till syng this lay quhilk folowand ye may here:	*song which following; hear*

	"Constrenyt hart, bylappit in distres,	*Confined heart, enfolded*
	Groundit in wo and full of hevynes	*Fixed*
	Complene thy paynfull caris infinyte,	
610	Bewale this warldis frele unstedfastnes	*frail*
	Havand regrait sen gone is thy glaidnes	*regret; happiness*
	And all thy solace returnyt in dispyte.	*pleasure turned back; spite*
	O cative thrall involupit in syte,	*slave; enwrapped in sorrow*
	Confesse thy fatale wofull wrechitnes,	*fated; wretchedness*
615	Divide in twane and furth diffound all tyte	*in half; pour out at once*
	Aggrevance gret in miserabill endyte.	*pitiable poetry*

"My crewell fait, subjectit to penance,　　　　*harsh fate, predisposed to suffering*
Predestinat sa void of all plesance,　　　　　　　　　*Destined; empty*
Has every greif amyd myn hart ingrave.　　　　　*grief; upon; engraved*
620　The slyd inconstant destany or chance　　　　　　　　*slippery*
Unequaly doith hyng in thair ballance　　　　　　　　　*hangs*
My demeritis and gret dolour I have.
This purgatory redowblys all the lave.　　　　*redoubles; remainder*
Ilk wycht has sum weilfare at obeysance　　*Everyone; prosperity at command*
625　Save me, bysnyng, that may na grace ressave.　　*monstrosity; receive*
Dede, the addresse and do me to my grave.　　*Death, get ready and send*

"Wo worth sik strang mysforton anoyus　　　　*Cursed be; troublesome*
Quhilk has opprest my spretis maist joyus!　　　　　　*Which*
Wo worth this worldis freuch felicité!　　　　*Woe befall; brittle*
630　Wo worth my fervent diseis dolorus!　　　　　*burning disquiet*
Wo worth the wycht that is not pietuus　　　　*person; merciful*
Quhare the trespassor penitent thay se!
Wo worth this dede that dayly dois me de!　　　*death; makes me die*
Wo worth Cupid and wo worth fals Venus,
635　Wo worth thaym bayth, ay waryit mot thay be!　　　*accursed*
Wo worth thair court, and cursit destane!"　　　　*destiny*

Loude as I mocht in dolour al distrenyeit　　　*was able; gripped*
This lay I sayng and not a lettir fenyeit.　　*did not make up a letter*
Tho saw I Venus on hir lyp did byte
640　And all the court in hast thair horsys renyeit　　　*reined in*
Proclamand loude, "Quhare is yone poid that plenyeit　*Where is that toad*
Quhilk deth diservis committand sik dispite?"　*Who deserves death [for]; offence*
Fra tre to tre thay serchyng but respyte　　*From tree; without rest*
Quhill ane me fand, quhilk said in greif disdenyeit,　*found; in scornful spite*
645　"Avant, velane, thou reclus imperfyte!"　　*Come out, churl; faulty hermit*

All in ane fevyr out of my muskan bowr　　*fever; decayed bower*
On knees I crap and law for feare did lowr.　　*crept; low; grovel*
Than all the court on me thayr hedis schuke,　　*shook their heads at me*
Sum glowmand grym, sum grinand with vissage sowr.　*scowling grimly; snarling*
650　Sum in the nek gave me feil dyntis dour.　　　*many heavy blows*
"Pluk at the craw," thay cryit, "deplome the ruke!　*Pluck the crow; deplume; rook*
Pulland my hare, with blek my face they bruke.　　*blacking; besmear*

Skrymmory Fery gaif me mony a clowr. *bump on the head*
For Chyppynuty full oft my chaftis quuke. *Because of; my jaws rattled*

655 With payne, torment thus in thayr teynfull play, *tormented; spiteful game*
Till Venus, bund, they led me furth the way *To; tied up*
Quhilk than wes set amyd a golden chare, *Who; upon*
And so confoundit into that fell affray *abashed; ruthless attack*
As that I micht consydyr thair array.
660 Me thocht the feild, ovirspred with carpetis fare, *covered*
Quhilk wes tofore brint, barrant, vile and bare, *formerly scorched, sterile*
Wox maist plesand, bot all, the suyth to say, *Became most pleasing; truth*
Micht not amese my grewous pane full sare. *lessen; grievous pain*

Entronit sat Mars, Cupyd and Venus.
665 Tho rais a clerk wes clepit Varius *Then arose; [who] was named*
Me tyl accusyng of a dedly cryme
And he begouth and red a dittay thus: *began; indictment*
"Thou wikkyt catyve, wood and furious, *insane and demented*
Presumptuusly now at this present tyme
670 My lady here blasphemed in thy ryme.
Hir sonne, hir self and hir court amorus
For till betrais awatit here sen prime." *betray lay in wait; sunrise*

Now God Thow wate, me thocht my fortune fey. *it seemed to me; was doomed*
Wyth quakand voce and hart cald as a key *quivering; cold*
675 On kneys I knelyt and mercy culd implore, *implored*
Submyttand me but ony langer pley *without longer plea*
Venus mandate and plesour till obey. *command*
Grace wes denyit and my travel forlore *my effort wasted*
For scho gaif chargis till procede as before.
680 Than Varius spak rycht stoutly me till fley, *to terrify me*
Injonand silence tyll ask grace ony more.[1]

He demandit myn answere, quhat I sayd,
Than as I mocht with curage all mysmaid *upset*
Fra tyme I undirstude na mare supple, *Once; [there'd be] no further aid*

---

[1] *Imposing silence (forbidding me) to ask again for mercy*

685	Sore abasyt, belive I thus out braid:	*abashed; at once; burst out*
	"Set of thir pointis of cryme now on me laid	*Suppose these particular aspects*
	I may me quyte giltles in verité,	*acquit myself; in truth*
	Yit fyrst, agane the juge quhilk here I se,	*against the judge whom*
	This inordenat court and proces quaid	*irregular; improper proceedings*
690	I wyll object for causys twa or thre."	

	Inclynand law, quod I with pietuus face,	*Bowing low; mournful*
	"I me defend, Madame plesyt your grace."	*if it please*
	"Say on," quod sche, than said I thus but mare:	*without delay*
	"Madame, ye may not syt in till this cace	*preside over*
695	For ladyis may be jugis in na place	*judges*
	And, mare attour, I am na seculare.	*furthermore; layman*
	A spirituall man (thocht I be void of lare)	*although; bereft of learning*
	Clepyt I am, and aucht my lyvys space	*I am called; during my life*
	To be remyt till my juge ordinare.	*handed over to my proper judge*

700	"I yow beseik, Madame with byssy cure,	*beseech; diligent attention*
	Till gyf ane gracius interlocuture	*a favorable interim judgment*
	On thir exceptionys now proponyt late."	*these pleas just put forward*
	Than suddanly Venus (I yow assure)	
	Deliverit sone and with a voce so sture	*Decided at once; forceful*
705	Answeryt thus: "Thow subtyle smy, God wait!	*wretch, God knows*
	Quhat wenys thou? Till degraid myne hie estate,	*What are you aiming at*
	Me till declyne as juge, curst creature?	*refuse to acknowledge as judge*
	It beis not so. The game gois othir gate.	*shall not be; another way*

	"As we the fynd, thow sall thoill jugement.	*As we determine you [to be]; suffer*
710	Not of a clerk we se the represent	*Nothing; you stand for*
	Save onely falsshed and dissaitfull talys.	*deceitful*
	Fyrst quhen thow come, with hart and hail entent	*when; whole intention*
	Thow the submyttit till my commaundement.	
	Now, now, thairof me think to sone thow falys!	*too soon you fail*
715	I weyn nathyng bot foly that the alys.	*reckon; ails you*
	Ye clerkis bene in subtyle wordis quent	*artful; ingenious*
	And in the deid als scharpe as ony snalys.	*deed; eager; snails*

	"Ye bene the men bewrays my commandis.	*[who] malign*
	Ye bene the men distrublys my servandis.	*molest*

36

720	Ye bene the men with wikkyt wordis fele	*many*
	Quhilk blasphemys fresch lusty yong gallandis	*youths*
	That in my servyce and retenew standis.	*retinue*
	Ye bene the men that clepys yow so lele	*who call yourselves so loyal*
	With fals behest quhill ye your purpose stele,	*false assurance; contrive*
725	Syne ye forswere baith body, treuth and handis,	*person, loyalty; undertakings*
	Ye bene sa fals. Ye can no word consele!	*conceal*

	"Have doyn," quod sche, "syr Varius. Alswyith	*Have done; Immediately*
	Do writ the sentence. Lat this cative kyith	*wretch give proof*
	Gyf our power may demyng his mysdeid."	*Whether; pass sentence upon*
730	Than God Thow wait gyf that my spreit wes blyith!	*know; blithe*
	The feverus hew in till my face dyd myith	*in my face; show*
	All my male eys for swa the horribill dreid	*distress; so; dread*
	Hail me ovyrset I mycht not say my creid.	*Completely overcame me; Creed*
	For feir and wo within my skyn I wryith.	*fear; squirm*
735	I mycht not pray, forsuyth, thocht I had neid.	*indeed, although*

	Yit of my deth I set not half a fle.	*death; flea*
	For gret effere me thocht na pane to die	*dread; no pain*
	But sore I dred me for sum othyr jape	*trick*
	That Venus suld throw hir subtillyté	*artifice*
740	In till sum bysnyng best transfigurat me	*monstrous beast transform*
	As in a bere, a bair, ane oule, ane ape.	*into a bear; boar; owl*
	I traistit so for till have bene myschaip	*expected; deformed*
	That oft I wald my hand behald to se	*would examine my hand*
	Gyf it alteryt, and oft my vissage grape.	*was altered; laid hold of my face*

745	Tho I revolvit in my mynd anone	*considered; at once*
	Quhow that Diane transformyt Acteone	
	And Juno eik as for a kow gert kepe	*cow; ordered to be kept*
	The fare Io that lang wes wo begone —	*fair; long was miserable*
	Argos hir yymmyt that eyn had mony one	*guarded; eyes*
750	Quhom at the last Mercurius gert slepe	*Whom; caused to sleep*
	And hir delyverit of that danger depe.	*rescued*
	I remembrit also quhow in a stone	*how into*
	The wyfe of Loth ichangit sore did wepe.	*Lot*

	I umbethocht quhow Jove and ald Saturn	*considered*

755	In tyll a wolf thay did Lycaon turn	*Into*
	And quhow the mychty Nabugodonosore	*Nebuchadnezzar*
	In bestly forme did on the feild sudjourn	*dwell*
	And for his gilt wes maid to wepe and murn.	*guilt*
	Thir feirfull wondris gart me dreid ful sore	*These; made me dread*
760	For by exemplys oft I herd tofore	
	He suld bewar that seys his fallow spurn:	*companion stumble*
	Myschans of ane suld be ane otheris lore.	*Misfortune; instruction*
	And rolland thus in divers fantasyis,	*contemplating; fanciful notions*
	Terribil thochtis oft my hert did gryis	*cause to shudder*
765	For all remeid wes alterit in dispare.	*turned into*
	Thare wes na hope of mercy till devyis.	*invent*
	Thare wes na wycht my frend be na kyn wyis.	*no one; by any means*
	Alhalely the court wes me contrare.	*Entirely; against me*
	Than wes all maist wryttyn the sentence sare.	*just about; heavy*
770	My febyll mynd, seand this gret suppris,	*expecting; shock*
	Wes than of wit and every blys full bare.	*barren*

The Seconde Parte

	Lo, thus amyd this hard perplexité	*intense bewilderment*
	Awaytand ever quhat moment I suld de	*Anticipating; die*
	Or than sum new transfiguration,	*Or else*
775	He quhilk that is eternall verité,	*truth*
	The glorious Lord ryngand in personis thre,	*reigning; three persons (the Trinity)*
	Providit has for my salvation	*Has supplied means for my deliverance*
	Be sum gude spretis revelation	*Because of some good spirit's disclosure*
	Quhilk intercessioun maid, I traist, for me.	*Who interceded; on my behalf*
780	I foryet all imagination.	*forgot; fanciful notion(s)*
	All hail my dreid I tho foryet in hy	*Altogether; then forgot in haste*
	And all my wo, bot yit I wyst not quhy,	*I did not know why*
	Save that I had sum hope till be relevyt.	*to be rescued*
	I rasyt than my vissage hastely	*raised then my face*
785	And with a blenk anone I did espy	*glance; see*
	A lusty sycht quhilk nocht my hart engrevit,	*sight; did not vex my heart*
	A hevinly rout out throw the wod eschevyt	*company emerged from the forest*

Of quhame the bonty, gyf I not deny, — *excellence; if I do not contradict*
Uneth may be intill ane scripture brevit. — *Hardly; text recorded*

790 With lawrere crownyt in robbis syd all new, — *laurel; long robes*
Of a fassoun and all of stedfast hew, — *Of one style; unvarying hue*
Arrayit weil, a court I saw cum nere — *Well decked out; approach*
Of wyse degest eloquent fathers trew — *dignified; honorable*
And plesand ladyis quhilkis fresch bewtie schew, — *who displayed a youthful beauty*
795 Syngand softly full swete on thair manere — *in*
On poete wyse all divers versis sere, — *After the manner of a poet; variously*
Historyis gret in Latyne toung and Grew — *Narratives; Greek*
With fresche endyt and soundis gude till here. — *new style; good to hear*

And sum of thaym *ad lyram* playit and sang — *some of them; on the lyre*
800 So plesand vers quhill all the rochys rang, — *until; rocks*
Metyr Saphik and also elygee. — *Sapphic and also elegiac meter*
Thair instrumentis all maist wer fydlys lang — *for the most part; monocords*
Bot with a string quhilk nevyr ane wreist yeid wrang. — *tuning-peg went wrong*
Sum had ane harpe and sum a fair psaltree; — *psaltery*
805 On lutis sum thair accentis subtelle — *strumming skillfully*
Devydyt weil and held the mesure lang — *Subdivided; kept to the larger rhythm*
In soundis swete of plesand melodie.

The ladyis sang in vocis dulcorate — *sweet voices*
Facund epistillis quhilkis quhilum Ovid wrate — *Eloquent; long ago; wrote*
810 As Phillys Quene send till Duke Demophon — *sent*
And of Pennolepe the gret regrate — *long letter of complaint*
Send till hir lord, sche dowtyng his estate, — *not knowing his condition*
That he at Troy suld losyt be or tone. — *killed or imprisoned*
How Acontus till Cedippa anone — *to; in haste*
815 Wrate his complaint thair hard I weil, God wate, — *Wrote; heard; knows*
With othir lusty myssyvis mony one. — *letters*

I had gret wondir of thair layis sere — *various songs*
Quhilkis in that arte mycht have na way compere — *have in no way an equal*
Of castis quent, rethorik colouris fyne[1]

---

[1] *In subtle turns of phrase, sophisticated devices of rhetoric*

39

820	So poete-lyk in subtyle fair manere	
	And elaquent fyrme cadens regulere.	*steady, regular rhythm*
	Thair vayage furth contenand rycht as lyne	*continuing straight as a line*
	With sang and play, as sayd is, so dyvine,	
	Thay fast approchyng to the place well nere	*approach*
825	Quhare I wes torment in my gastly pyne.	

	And as the hevynly sort now nomynate	*band just referred to*
	Removyt furth on gudly wyse thair gate	*Went forwards; their way*
	Towert the court quhilk wes tofore expremit,	*which was previously described*
	My curage grew, for quhat cause I not wate	*I did not know*
830	Save that I held me payit of thayr estate;	*considered myself pleased by*
	And thay wer folk of knawledge as it semit,	
	Als in til Venus court full fast thay demit,	*Since; expressed opinions*
	Sayand, "Yone lusty rout wyll stop our mate	*This fine company; our fellow*
	Till justefy thys bisning quhilk blasphemit.	*To condemn; monster who*

835	"Yone is," quod they, "the court rethoricall	
	Of polit termys, sang poeticall	*elegant words, song*
	And constand ground of famus historyis swete.	*fixed foundation; stories*
	Yone is the facund well celestiall.	*heavenly source of inspiration*
	Yone is the fontayn and origynall	*fountain; origin*
840	Quharefra the well of Helicon dois flete.	*Wherefrom; flow*
	Yone ar the folkis that comfortes every sprete	*soul*
	Be fyne delyte and dyte angelicall	*angelic style of writing*
	Causand gros lede all of maist gudnes glete.	*coarse language; glitter*

	"Yone is the court of plesand stedfastnes.	*(see note)*
845	Yone is the court of constant merynes.	
	Yone is the court of joyus disciplyne	
	Quhilk causys folk thair purpos till expres	*their intention*
	In ornat wyse provocand with gladnes,	*manner inspiring*
	All gentyll hartis to thare lare inclyne.	*pay attention to their erudition*
850	Every famus poet men may devyne	*conceive of*
	Is in yone rout. Lo yondir thair Prynces,	*that company; Princess*
	Thespis, the mothyr of the Musis Nyne,	

	"And nixt hir syne hir douchter fyrst byget,	*her eldest daughter*
	Lady Cleo, quhilk craftely dois set	*Clio; skilfully writes out*

855 Historiis ald lyk as thay wer present,   *Ancient stories*
     Euterpe eik, quhilk dayly dois hir det   *also; does her duty*
     In dulce blastis of pipis swete but let;   *gentle; without cease*
     The thyrd systir, Thalia, diligent
     In wanton wryt, and cronikillis doith imprent;   *writings about love*
860 The ferd endityth, oft with chekis wet,   *The fourth writes*
     Sare tragedyis, Melphomyne the gent;   *Bitter; Melpomene the noble*

     "Tarpsychore the fyft with humyll soun   *Terpsichore; soft sound*
     Makis on psaltreis modolatioun;   *melody*
     The sext, Erato, lyk thir luffirs wylde   *these insane lovers*
865 Will syng, play, dans and leip baith up and doune.   *leap*
     Polimnya, the sevynt Muse of renoun,   *Polyhymnia*
     Ditis thir swete rethorik cullouris mylde   *Writes; devices of rhetoric*
     Quhilkis ar so plesand baith to man and chylde;
     Uranya, the aucht and sistir schene,   *Urania; eighth; fair*
870 Wrytis the hevyn and sternys all bedene;   *stars at once*

     "The nynt, quham till nane othir is compere,   *ninth, to whom no other is equal*
     Caliope, that lusty lady clere,   *fair*
     Of quham the bewtye and the worthynes   *From whose beauty and excellence*
     The vertuys gret schynis baith far and nere,   *The power*
875 For sche of nobillis fatis hes the stere   *nobles' fates has control*
     Till wryt thair worschyp, victory and prowes   *To write; honor*
     In kyngly style, quhilk dois thair fame encres   *causes their fame to increase*
     Clepyt in Latyne *heroicus,* but were,   *Called; epic without doubt*
     Cheif of al wryt lyk as scho is maistres.

880 "Thir Musis nyne, lo yondir may ye se   *These*
     With fresch Nymphis of watir and of see,
     And Phanee, ladyis of thir templis ald,   *Fauns (see note)*
     Pyerides, Dryades, Saturee,   *Satyrs*
     Neriedes, Aones, Napee,   *Napaeae*
885 Of quham the bontyis nedis not be tald."   *good qualities*
     Thus dempt the court of Venus monyfald   *considered; diverse*
     Quhilk speche refreschyt my perplexité,   *relieved*
     Rejosand weil my sprete afore wes cald.   *spirit [which] before*

     The suddand sycht of that fyrme court foresaid

890	Recomfort weil my hew tofore wes faid.	*Restored; complexion [which]; pale*
	Amyd my brest the joyus heit redoundyt	*flowed back*
	Behaldand quhow the lusty Musys raid,	*Beholding how; rode*
	And al thair court quhilk wes so blyith and glaid,	
	Quhois merynes all hevynes confoundyt.	*gloominess overcame*
895	Thair saw I, weil in poetry ygroundyt,	*trained*
	The gret Homere, quhilk in Grew langage said	*Greek; spoke*
	Maist eloquently, in quham all wyt aboundyt.	

	Thare wes the gret Latyn Virgillyus,	*Virgil*
	The famus fathir poet Ovidius,	*Ovid*
900	Ditis, Daris, and eik the trew Lucane.	*Dictys Cretensis; Dares Phrygius; Lucan*
	Thare wes Plautus, Pogius, Parsius.	*Poggio Bracciolini; Persius*
	Thare wes Terens, Donat, and Servius,	*Terence; Aelius Donatus*
	Francys Petrark, Flakcus Valeriane.	*Petrarch; Valerius Flaccus*
	Thare wes Ysop, Caton, and Alane.	*Aesop; Dionysius Cato; Alain de Lille*
905	Thare wes Galterus and Boetius.	*Gautier de Châtillon; Boethius*
	Thare wes also the gret Quintilliane.	*Quintilian*

	Thare wes the satyr poete Juvinale.	*Juvenal*
	Thare wes the mixt and subtell Marciale.	*versatile; Martial*
	Of Thebes bruyt thare wes the poete Stace.	*fame; Statius*
910	Thare wes Faustus and Laurence of the vale,	*Fausto Andrelini; Lorenzo Valla*
	Pomponeus quhais fame of late, sans fale,	*Giulio Pomponio Leto; without fail*
	Is blawin wyd throw every realme and place.	
	Thare wes the morale wyse poete Orace,	*Horace*
	With mony other clerkis of gret avayle.	*great benefit*
915	Thare wes Brunell, Claudyus, and Bocace.	*Leonardo Bruni; Claudian; Boccaccio*

	So gret a pres of pepill drew us nere	*crowd; near us*
	The hunder part thare namys is not here.	*hundredth*
	Yit thare I saw of Brutus Albion	*Britain*
	Goffryd Chaucere, as *A per se*, sance pere	*the letter A, without equal*
920	In his wulgare, and morell John Gowere.	*vernacular*
	Lydgat the monk raid musand him allone.	*pondering by himself*
	Of this natioun I knew also anone	*Scotland; at once*
	Gret Kennedy and Dunbar, yit undede,	*alive*
	And Quyntyne with ane huttok on his hede.	*(see note)*

925	Howbeit I couth declare and weil endyte	*Even though; compose*
	The bonteis of that court, dewlye to wryt	*excellences; in due form*
	Wer ovir prolyxt, transcendyng myne engyne.	*lengthy; powers of invention*
	Twychand the proces of my panefull syte:	*Concerning; course; grief*
	Belive I saw thir lusty Musys quhyte	*white Muses*
930	With all thair route towart Venus declyne	*company; turn*
	Quhare Cupyd sat with hir in trone divyne,	*throne*
	I standand bundyn in a sory plyte	*tied up; sorry condition*
	Byddand thair grace or than the dedly pyne.	*Awaiting; mercy or else; torment*
	Straucht til the Quene sammyn thir Musis raid,	*Straight; together*
935	Maist eloquently thare salutationys maid.	
	Venus agane yald thaym thair salusyng	*returned their greeting*
	Rycht reverently, and on hir fete upbraid,	*got up*
	Besekand thaym to lycht. "Nay, nay," thay said,	*Beseeching; dismount*
	"We may as here make na langer tariyng."	*delay*
940	Caliope, maist facund and bening,	*eloquent and gracious*
	Inquyryt Venus what wicht had hir mismaid	*Asked; person; upset*
	Or wes the cause thair of hir sudjournyng.	*temporary stay*
	"Syster," sayd scho, "behald that bysnyng schrew.	*monstrous rascal*
	A subtyle smye — considyr weil his hew —	*sly wretch; hue (see note)*
945	Standis thair bond," and bykkynit hir to me.	*directed her attention*
	"Yone cative hes blasphemyt me of new	*just now*
	For tyl degraid and do my fame adew;	*cause my good name to depart*
	A laithly ryme dispitefull, subtelle	*disgusting, insulting rhyme, cunningly*
	Compelit hes, rehersand loud on hie	*Composed, reciting out loud*
950	Sclander, dispite, sorow and wallaway	*lamentation*
	To me, my sonne and eike my court for ay.	*Against; also; forever*
	"He has deservit deth — he salbe dede —	*shall be dead*
	And we remane forsuith in to this stede	*remain; indeed in this place*
	Till justefy that rebell renygate."	*condemn; renegade*
955	Quod Caliope, "Sister, away all fede.	*hostility*
	Quhy suld he de? Quhy suld he leis his hede?	*die; lose*
	To sla him for sa small a cryme, God wate,	*slay; knows*
	Greter degradyng wer to your estate	*Greater reproach; high rank*
	All out than wes his sclander or sich plede.	*Altogether; such controversy*
960	Quhow may a fule your hie renoun chakmate?	*How; checkmate*

"Quhat of his lak? Your fame so wyd is blaw,   *so far and wide is blown*
Your excellens maist peirles is so knaw,   *peerless; well-known*
Na wrichis word ay depare your hie name.   *wretch's; injure*
Gyf me his lyfe and modefy the law
965   For on my hed he standis now sic aw   *in such fear*
That he sall eft disserve nevir mare blame.   *afterwards*
Not of his dede ye may report but schame.   *Nothing*
In recompence of this mysyttand saw   *unbecoming speech*
He sall your hest in every part proclame."   *command*

970   Than Lord quhow glad becam my febil gost!
My curage grew, the quhilk afore wes lost,   *which before*
Seand I had so gret ane advocate   *Seeing*
That expertly, but prayer, pryce or cost,   *without request*
Opteynit had my frewel accion all most   *Won; futile legal case*
975   Quhilk wes afore perist and desolate.   *failed and abandoned*
This quhyil Venus stude, in ane study strate,   *Meanwhile; sudden doubt*
Bot fynally scho schew till all the ost   *indicated to all the company*
Scho wald do grace and be not obstinate.   *show mercy*

"I wyll," said sche, "have mercy and pyete,   *pity*
980   Do slake my wreth, and lat all rancour be.   *Cause my wrath to diminish*
Quhare is mare vice than till be ovir cruel
And specially in wemen sic as me?
A lady — fy! — that usis tirranne   *tyranny*
No woman is, rather a serpent fell.   *fierce*
985   A vennamus dragon or a devill of hell   *(see note)*
Is na compare to the inequyte   *unrighteousness*
Of bald wemen, as thir wyse clerkis tell.   *arrogant*

"Gret God diffend I suld be ane of tho   *forbid; should; those*
Quhilk of thare fede and malyce nevir ho.   *Who; hostility; cease*
990   Out on sik gram! I wyll serve na repreif.   *wrath; deserve; reproof*
Caliope, sistir," said til Venus tho,   *Venus said to her then*
"At your request this wreche sall frely go.   *wretch*
Heir I remyt his trespas, and all greif   *pardon his offence; injury*
Salbe foryet swa he wil say sum breif   *Shall be forgotten as long as; letter*
995   Or schort ballat in contrare pane and wo   *in opposition to*
Tuychand my laud and his plesand releif.   *Concerning; praise*

"And secundly the nixt resonabil command
Quhilk I him charge: se that he not ganestand.   *resist*
On thir conditions, sister, at your requeist
1000   He sall go fre." Quod Caliope inclynand,   *bowing*
"Grant mercy, sister, I oblys by my hand   *pledge*
He sall observe in al poyntis your beheist."   *command*
Than Venus bad do slake sone my arreist   *ordered my arrest be ended at once*
Belyve I wes releschit of every band,   *Straightaway; released*
1005   Uprais the court and all the perlour ceist.   *discussion ceased*

Tho sat I doun lawly upon my kne   *humbly*
At command of prudent Caliope,
Yeildand Venus thankis a thousand sith   *Offering; times*
For sa hie frendschip and mercyfull pieté,   *such*
1010   Excelland grace and gret humanyté
The quhilk to me, trespassour, did scho kyth.   *which; show*
"I the forgeve," quod sche. Than wes I blyth.
Doun on a stok I set me suddanlye   *tree-stump*
At hir command and wrate this lay als swyth: *wrote; song; just as fast*

1015   "Unwemmyt wit, deliverit of dangear,   *Unblemished; rescued from*
Maist happely preservit fra the snare,   *fortunately*
Releschit fre of servyce and bondage,   *Released unconstrained by*
Expell dolour, expell diseyses sare,   *sorrow; bitter sufferings*
Avoyd displesour, womentyng and care,   *lamenting*
1020   Ressave plesans and do thy sorowe swage,   *let your sorrow be lessened*
Behald thy glaid fresche lusty grene curage,   *spirits*
Rejois amyd thir lovers lait and air,   *continually*
Provyde a place till plant thy tendir age   *to*
Quhair thou in joy and plesour may repair.   *resort*

1025   "Quha is in welth, quha is weill fortunat,   *Who*
Quha is in peace, dissoverit from debbat,   *set apart from conflict*
Quha levys in hop, quha levys in esperance,   *lives in hope*
Quha standis in grace, quha standis in ferme estat,   *assured*
Quha is content, rejosyt air and lat,   *continually*
1030   Or quha is he that fortune doith avance   *causes to prosper*
Bot thow, that is replenyst with plesance?   *fully endowed with*
Thow hes comfort, all weilfare dilligat;   *delightful prosperity*

Thow hes gladnes; thow hes the happy chance;
Thow hes thy wyll: now be not dissolat.   *forlorn*

1035 "Incres in myrthfull consolatioun,
In joyus swete ymaginatioun,
Habond in luif of purifyit amouris   *Abound; love*
With diligent trew deliberatioun,   *secure thoughts*
Rendir lovyngis for thy salvatioun   *praises*
1040 Till Venus, and ondir hir gard all houris   *under her protection always*
Rest at all ease, but sair or sytful schouris.   *without bouts of pain or bitterness*
Abyde in quyet, maist constant weilfare.
Be glaid and lycht now in thy lusty flouris,   *cheerful; in your fine vigour*
Unwemmyt wyt, delyverit of dangare."   *Unstained; rescued from*

1045 This lay wes red in oppyn audience
Of the Musis, and in Venus' presence.
"I stand content: thow art obedient,"
Quod Caliope, my campion and defence.   *protector*
Venus sayid, eik, it wes sum recompence   *also*
1050 For my trespas I wes so penytent,
And with that word all sodanly sche went.   *departed*
In ane instant scho and hir court wes hence,
Yit still abayd thir Musis on the bent.   *lingered; the field*

Inclynand than, I sayd, "Caliope   *Bowing*
1055 My protector, my help and my supple,   *means of support*
My soverane lady, my redemptioun,
My mediatour quhen I wes dampnyt to de,   *condemned to die*
I sall beseik the Godly Majeste   *request from God*
Infynyt thankis, laud and benysoun
1060 Yow till acquyte, accordyng your renoun.   *to repay, as befits*
It langyth not my possibillite   *It is not within my power*
Till recompence ten part of this gwardoun.   *a tenth part of this reward*

"Glore, honour, laude and reverence condyng   *praise; suitable*
Quha may foryeild yow of so hie a thyng?   *Who; recompense you for*
1065 And in that part your mercy I implore
Submyttand me my lyftyme induring   *myself; for the length of*
Your plesour and mandate till obeysyng."   *command to obey*

46

"Silence," said scho, "I have eneuch heirfore.   *enough on this account*
I will thow passe and vissy wondris more."   *proceed; view*
1070 Than scho me hes betaucht in kepyng   *entrusted me into the care*
Of a swete Nymphe, maist faythfull and decore.   *beautified*

Ane hors I gat, maist rychely besene,   *decked out*
Was harnyst all with wodbynd levis grene.   *woodbind leaves*
On the same sute the trappuris law doun hang.   *horse-cloths hung down low*
1075 Ovir hym I straid at command of the Quene,   *Upon; mounted*
Tho sammyn furth we rydyng all bedene   *Then together; rode at once*
Als swyft as thocht with mony a mery sang.   *As; thought*
My Nymphe alwayis convoyt me of thrang,   *guided; away from the crowd*
Amyd the Musys till se quhat thay wald mene,   *Amongst; would intend*
1080 Quhilkis sang and playt bot nevir a wrest yeid wrang.   *tuning-peg went wrong*

Throw cuntreis seir, holtis and rochys hie,   *many countries; forests; rocks*
Ovir valys, planys, woddis, wally se,   *valleys, plains; rough sea*
Ovir fludis fare and mony strate montane   *fine rivers; steep*
We wer caryit in twynklyng of ane e.   *eye*
1085 Our horssis flaw and raid nocht, as thocht me,   *did not go on foot, it seemed to me*
Now out of France tursyt in Tuskane,   *carried off into Tuscany*
Now out of Flandris heich up in Almane,   *Flanders far up; South Germany*
Now in till Egypt, now in Ytalie,   *Italy*
Now in the realme of Trace and now in Spane.   *Thrace; Spain*

1090 The montayns we passit of all Garmanie,   *Germany*
Ovir Appenynus devydand Ytalie,   *the Appenines dividing*
Ovir Ryne, the Pow and Tiber fludis fare,   *Rhine; Po; rivers [we] travel*
Ovir Alpheus, by Pyes the ryche citie,   *(see note)*
Undir the erth that entres in the see,   *That flows underground into the sea*
1095 Ovir Ron, ovir Sane, ovir France and eik ovir Lare   *Rhone; Seine; also; Loire*
And ovir Tagus, the goldin sandyt ryvare.
In Thessaly we passit the mont Oethe,   *Oite*
And Hercules in sepulture fand there.   *found*

Thare went we ovir the ryver Peneyus.   *Peneus*
1100 In Secil eik we passyt the mont Tmolus,   *Cilicia*
Plenyst with saphron, huny and with wyne;   *Flourishing; saffron; honey*
The twa toppyt famus Pernasus;   *twin-peaked; Parnassus*

In Trais we went out ovir the mont Emus   *Thrace; Haemus*
Quhare Orphius lerit his armony maist fyne,   *Where Orpheus learned*
1105 Ovir Carmelus, quhare twa prophetis devyne   *Mount Carmel*
Remanyt, Helyas and Heliseus,   *Dwelt, Elijah and Elisha*
Fra quhome the Ordur of Carmelitis come syne.   *Carmelites came afterwards*

And nixt untill the land of Amyson,   *Amazonia*
In hast we past the flude Termodyon   *Thermodon*
1110 And ovir the huge hill that hecht Mynas.   *is named Mimas*
We raid the hill of Bachus, Citheron,   *rode over; Bacchus, Cithaeron*
And Olympus, the mont of Massidon,   *Macedonia*
Quhilk semys heich up in the hevyn to pas.   *high; to stretch*
In that countre, we raid the flude Melas
1115 Quhais watter makith quhite scheip blak anon.   *white sheep; at once*
In Europe, eik, we raid the flud Thanas.   *also; the Don River*

We raid the swyft revere Sparthiades,   *Sperchius*
The flud of Surry Achicorontes,   *Syria; Orontes*
The hill so full of wellis clepit Yda,   *named Ida*
1120 Armany hillis and flude Eufrates, *The hills of Armenia; Euphrates River*
The fluid of Nyle, the pretius flude Ganges,   *Nile; rich*
The hyl of Secyle, ay-byrnand Ethna,   *Sicily, ever-burning Etna*
And ovir the mont of Frygy, Dindama,   *Phrygia; Dindymon*
Hallowit in honour of the Modir Goddes.   *Consecrated; Cybele*
1125 Cauld Cacasus we passit, in Sythia.   *Caucasus; Scythia*

We passyt the fludis of Tygris and Phison,   *Tigris*
Of Trace the riveris Hebrun and Strymon, *Thrace; Hebrus; Strimon*
The mont of Modyn and the flud Jordane,   *River Jordan*
The facund well and hill of Elicon,   *overflowing; Helicon*
1130 The mont Erix, the well of Acheron,   *Eryx*
Baith didicat to Venus en certane.   *dedicated; indeed*
We past the hill and desert of Lybane,   *Lebanon*
Ovir mont Cinthus, quhare God Appollo schone   *Cynthus*
Straucht to the Musis Caballyne fontane.   *Directly; Hippocrene*

1135 Besyde that cristall strand swete and degest   *stream; calm*
Them till repois, thayr hors refresch and rest,   *repose*
Alychtit doun thir Musis clere of hew. *Dismounted; fresh of complexion*

The cumpany all halely, lest and best,	*altogether, lowest and highest*
Thrang to the well tyl drink, quhilk ran southwest	*Thronged*
1140 Throw out a meid quhare alkyn flouris grew.	*meadow; all kinds of*
Amang the layf ful fast I did persew	*rest; hurry*
Tyll drynk, bot sa the gret pres me opprest	*crowd*
That of the watir I micht never tast a drew.	*drop*

Our hors pasturyt in a plesand plane	
1145 Law at the fute of a fare grene mountane	
Amyd a meid schadowed with cedir treys,	*meadow; trees*
Save fra al heit thare micht we weil remane,	*Safe; heat*
All kynd of herbis, flouris, frute and grane	
With every growand tre thair men micht cheis.	*might [wish to] select*
1150 The byrriall stremys rynnand ovyr sterny greis	*crystal; glittering steps*
Maid sobir noys; the schaw dynnyt agane	*subdued sound; thicket resounded*
For byrdys sang and soundyng of the beis.	*With; bees*

The ladyis fare on divers instrumentys	*fair*
Went playand, syngand, dansand ovir the bentis.	*fields*
1155 Ful angelyk and hevynly wes thair soun.	
Quhat creatour amid his hart imprentis	*created being; imprints*
The fresche bewty, the gudly representis,	*appearances*
The mery spech, fare havinges, hie renoun	*fine manners*
Of thaym wald set a wyse man halfe in swoun.	
1160 Thair womanlynes writhyt the elementis,	*unsettled (see note)*
Stonyst the hevyn and all the erth adoun.	*Stunned; below*

The warld may not consydyr nor discryve	*account for*
The hevynly joy, the blys I saw belyve,	*at once*
So ineffabill, abone my wyt so hie	*above my understanding*
1165 I wyll na mare thairon my forhed ryve,	*no longer; overwork my mind*
But breifly furth my febill proces dryve.	*feeble discourse*
Law in the meid a palyeon pycht I se,	*Low; pavilion erected*
Maist gudlyest and rychest that myght be.	
My governour ofter than timys fyve	*guardian; more often*
1170 Untill that halde to pas commandit me.	*shelter; to go*

Swa fynally strycht to that rial steid	*directly; royal site*
In fallowschip with my leder I yeid.	*leader; went*

We entryt sone: the portar wes not thra;	*was not obstinate*
Thare wes na stoppyng, lang demand nor pleid.	*long interrogation; dispute*
1175 I knelyt law and onheldit my heid	*uncovered my head*
And tho I saw our Musis twa and twa	*then*
Sittand on deace, famylliaris to and fra	*dais; members of the household*
Servand thaym fast with epocres and meid,	*spiced wine; mead*
Dilligate meatis, daynteis sere alswa.	*Fine food, various dainties also*

1180 Grete wes the preis, the feist ryall to sene.	*crowd*
At ease thay eit with interludyis betwene,	*Informally; interludes between courses*
Gave problemys sere and mony fare demandis	*various puzzling questions*
Inquirand quha best in thair tymys had bene,	*who*
Quha traist lovers in lusty yeris grene;	*faithful; years of vigour and youth*
1185 Sum said this way, and sum thairto ganstandis.	*disagrees*
Than Caliope Ovid till appere commaundis:	*to come forth*
"My Clerk," quod scho, "of Registere, bedene	*official keeper of records, now*
Declare quha wer maist worthy of thair handis."	*who*

With lawrere crownyt, at hir commaundment	*laurel*
1190 Up stude this poet degest and eloquent	*dignified*
And schew the fetis of Hercules the strang,	*showed; feats*
Quhow he the grysly hellis houndis out rent,	*(see note)*
Slew lyonys, monstreis and mony fell serpent,	
And to the deth feil mychty giantis dang.	*many; struck*
1195 Of Thesyus eik he tald the weris lang	*also; wars*
Agane the quene Ypollita the swete	*Hippolyta*
And quhow he slew the Mynotaure in Crete;	

Of Persyus he tald the knychtly dedis	*Perseus*
Quhilk vincussyt (as men in Ovid redis)	*vanquished*
1200 Crewell tyrrantis and monsturis mony one;	
Of Dianis bore in Callydon the dredis,	*Diana's boar; Caledon; dangers*
Quhow throw a ladyis schot his sydis bledis —	*(Atalanta's) shot; his flanks bleed*
The bretheris deith and syne the systeris mone;	*lament (moan)*
He schew quhow Kyng Priamus sonne Ysacon	*Priam's; Aesacus*
1205 Efter his dede, body and all his wedis	*death; clothes*
In till a skarth transformyt wes anon;	*cormorant*

He schew at Troy quhat wyis the Grekis landis,	*in what manner*

Quhow fers Achylles stranglyt wyth his handis
The valyeant Cignus, Neptunus' sonne maist dere,   *Cygnus*
1210 Quhilk at Grekis aryvale on the strandis   *shores*
A thousand slew that day apon the sandis,
Faucht with Achill and blontit al his spere —   *blunted*
Na wapyn wes that micht him wond nor dere   *wound or harm*
Quhill Achalles bryst of his helm the bandis   *Until; ripped from; straps*
1215 And wyrryit hym be fors for all his fere.   *strangled; strength despite; companions*

He schew full mony transmutationis   *metamorphoses*
And wondirfull new figurationis   *forms*
Be hondris mo than I have here expremyt.   *hundreds more; described*
He tald of lovys meditacionis,   *discourses of love*
1220 The craft of love and the salvationis,   *deliverances [from love]*
Quhow that the furie lustis suld be flemyt.   *expelled*
Of divers other materis als he demyt   *gave judgment*
And be his prudent scharpe relationys   *acute statements*
He wes expart in all thyng, as it semyt.

1225 Up rais the gret Virgilius anone   *Virgil*
And playd the sportis of Daphnis and Coridon.   *pastimes*
Syne Therens come, and playit the commedy   *Then Terence came*
Of Permeno, Thrason and wyse Gnaton;   *Parmeno, Thraso; Gnatho*
Juvynale, lik a mower, hym allone,   *Juvenal; jester; by himself*
1230 Stud skornand every man as thay yeid by;   *mocking; went past*
Marcyall was cuyk, till rost, seith, fars or fry;   *Martial; cook; boil, stuff*
And Pogyus stude with mony gyrn and grone   *Poggio; sneer; groan*
On Laurence Valla spyttand and cryand "Fy!"   *spitting and crying*

With myrthys thus and meatis diligate   *entertainments; tasty dishes*
1235 Thir ladyis, festit accordyng thair estate,   *as suited their high rank*
Uprais at last, commandand till tranoynt.   *to rapidly get underway*
Retret wes blawyn lowd, and than God wate   *The signal for departure*
Men micht have sene swyft horssys halden hate   *ridden hard*
Schynand for swete as thay had bene anoynt.   *sweat; anointed*
1240 Of all that rout wes never a pryk disjoynt   *not a stride out of place*
For all our tary, and I, furth with my mate,   *Despite our sojourn*
Montyt on hors, raid sammyn in gude poynt.   *together; good array*

	Ovir many gudly plane we raid bedene,	*straightaway*
	The Vail of Ebron, the Campe Damascene,	*Vale of Hebron; Field of Damascus*
1245	Throw Josaphat and throw the lusty vail,	*Jehoshaphat; valley*
	Ovir watres wan, throw worthi woddis grene,	*dark (i.e., deep)*
	And swa at last in lyftyng up our eyne	
	We se the fynall end of our travail:	
	Amyd ane plane a plesand roch till wail.	*to choose*
1250	And every wycht fra we that sycht had sene,	*person once*
	Thankand gret God, thare hedis law devail.	*bow their heads down low*

	With syngyng, lauchyng, merines and play	*laughing, merriment*
	On till that roch we rydyng furth the way.	*rode*
	Now mare till writ for fere trymlys my pen.	*fear trembles*
1255	The hart may not thynk nor manis toung say,	
	The eyr not here nor yet the e se may,	*eye*
	It may not be ymagyned with men	*by men*
	The hevynly blys, the perfyte joy to ken	
	Quhilk now I saw. The hundreth part all day	*Which*
1260	I micht not schaw, thocht I had tonges ten.	*reveal even if*

	Thocht al my membris tongis were on raw	*Even if all my bodily parts; in a row*
	I wer not abill the thousandfald to schaw	*would not be able; thousandth part*
	Quhairfore I fere ocht forthirmare to wryte,	*fear; anything more*
	For quhiddir I this in saule or body saw	*whether*
1265	That wait I not, bot he that all duth knaw,	*That I do not know;*
	The gret God, wait in every thyng perfyt.	
	Eik gyf I wald this ʼavyssyon endyte	*if; write out*
	Janglaris suld it bakbyt and stand nane aw[1]	
	Cry out on dremes quhilkis ar not worth a myte!	*against; which*

1270	Sen thys til me all verite be kend	*is shown to me [to be] all truth*
	I reput bettir thus, till mak ane end	*I reckon [it]*
	Than ocht til say that suld herars engreve.	*to say anything; listeners annoy*
	On othir syd, thocht thay me vilepend,	*though they (i.e., the "janglers") vilify me*
	I considir prudent folk will commend	*reckon; extol*
1275	The verete, and sic janglyng rapreve.	*truth; such; condemn*

---

[1] *Chatterers would speak ill of it and show no hesitation (to)*

With quhais correction, support, and releve | *whose; assistance*
Furth till proceid this proces I pretend, | *I plan to carry this discourse forward*
Traistand in God my purpose till escheve. | *achieve*

Quhowbeit I may not every circumstance | *Even though*
1280 Reduce perfytly in rememorance, | *Recall; memory*
Myn ignorance yit sum part sal devyse | *nevertheless; retell*
Twychand this sycht of hevynly swete plesance. | *Concerning*
Now empty pen, wryt furth thy lusty chance, | *fine opportunity*
Schaw wondris fele, suppose thow be not wyse, | *many; even though*
1285 Be dilligent and rypely the avyse, | *maturely bethink yourself*
Be qwyke and scharpe, voydit of variance, | *free of inconstancy*
Be suete and cause not jentill hartis gryse. | *pleasing; to shudder*

The Thyrd Parte

Ye Musis nyne, be in myne adjutory | *come to my assistance*
That maid me se this blys and perfyte glory, | *Who enabled me to see*
1290 Teche me your facund castis eloquent, | *Teach; expressive devices of eloquence*
Len me a recent, scharp, fresch memory, | *Give; newly-made, discerning, vivid*
And caus me dewly til indyt this story. | *properly to record*
Sum gratius swetnes in my brest imprent | *imprint*
Till make the heraris bousum and attent, | *audience receptive and alert*
1295 Redand my wryt illumynyt with your lore, | *Reading; illumined; teaching*
Infynyt thankis rendrand yow thairfore. | *offering*

Now breifly to my purpose for til gone. | *directly; subject; to proceed*
About the hyll lay ways mony one, | *On all sides of the hill; paths*
And to the hycht bot a passage ingrave, | *to the top only one pathway carved out*
1300 Hewyn in the roch of slyde hard merbyll stone. | *Hewn; rock; slippery*
Aganne the sonne lyk as the glas it schone. | *Reflecting the sun*
Ascens wes hie and strait for till consave, | *difficult to grasp with the mind*
Yit than thir Musis, gudly and suave, | *But nevertheless; gracious*
Alychtyt doun and clam the roch in hy | *Dismounted; climbed; in haste*
1305 With all the route, outtane my Nynphe and I. | *company except*

Styl at the hillys fute we twa abaid. | *we two lingered*
Than suddandly my keper to me said,

53

"Ascend, galand!" Tho for fere I quuke.   *young gentleman; fear; shook*
"Be not effrayit," scho said, "be not mismaid,"   *afraid; disturbed*
1310   And with that word up the strait rod abraid.   *narrow path [she] sprang*
I followit fast; scho be the hand me tuke,
Yit durst I nevir, for dreid, behynde me luke.
With mekill pane thus clam we nere the hycht,   *great exertion; climbed*
Quhare suddandly I saw ane grysly sycht.

1315   As we approchit nere the hillis heid,   *top*
A terrible sewch — birnand in flawmys reid,   *gulf; burning with red flames*
Abhominable and hol as heill to se,   *cavernous as hell*
All full of bryntstane, pyk, and bulnyng leid,   *sulphur, tar, and boiling lead*
Quhair mony wrechit creatour lay deid,
1320   And miserable catywis yeland loude one hie —   *wretches yelling out loud*
I saw, quhilk den mycht wele comparit be
Till Xantus, the fluid of Troy so schill,   *Xanthus; river; chilling*
Byrnand at Venus hest, contrar Achill.   *command; in opposition to*

Amyd our passage lay this ugly sicht,   *Across our path; sight*
1325   Not brayd, but so horrible till eviry wicht   *wide; horrifying to every person*
That all the warld to pas it suld have dreid.   *would be afraid*
Wele I considerit nene upparmar I mycht,   *no further upwards could I go*
And to discend, sa hiddous wes the hicht   *height*
I durst not aventur for this erth on breid.[1]
1330   Trymland I stud, with teith chatterand gud speid.   *Trembling; at a fine pace*
My Nymphe beheld my cheir and said "Lat be: *noticed my face; Be still*
Thow sall not aill, and, lo, the caus," quod sche.   *You'll not be at risk; here's why*

"To me thow art commyt. I sall the keip.   *entrusted; shall protect you*
Thir pieteous pepill amyd theis laithly deip   *pitiful; this loathsome pit*
1335   War wrechis quhilkis in lusty yeris fair   *in the pleasant years of youth*
Pretendit thaym till hie honour to creip;   *Put themselves forward; proceed humbly*
Bot suddandly thay fell on sleuthfull sleip   *into slothful sleep*
Followand plesance, drynt in this loch of cair."   *pleasure; drowned; lake of sorrow*
And with that word sche hynt me by the hair,   *grabbed*
1340   Caryit me to the hillis hed anone   *top; at once*

---

[1] *I dared not attempt [it]; not for the whole world*

The Palis of Honoure

As Abacuk wes brocht in Babilone.   *Habakkuk; Babylon*

As we bene on the hie hill sittuate,   *While; were; located*
"Luke doun." quod scho, "Consave in quhat estat   *Imagine; condition*
Thy wrechyt warld thow may considdir now!"[1]
1345 At hir command, with mekill dreid, God wate,   *great fear; knows*
Out ovir the hill sa hiddous hie and strate   *horribly high and steep*
I blent adoun, and feld my body grow: *glanced; felt; shiver*
This brukkill erth, sa littyl to allow   *fragile world; reckon*
Me thocht I saw byrn in a fyry rage
1350 Of stormy see, quhilk mycht na maner swage.   *which would in no way subside*

That terribbill tempest, hiddous wallys huge   *waves*
Wer maist grysly for till behald or juge,
Quhare nothyr rest nor quyet mycht appere.   *Where*
Thare wes a peralus palyce, folk to luge.   *[in which] to house folk*
1355 Thare wes na help, support nor yet refuge.
Innowmerabill folk I saw flottrand in fere   *Innumerable; floundering together*
Quhilk peryst on the weltrand wallys were[2]
And secondly I saw a lusty barge   *fine ship*
Ovirset with seyes and mony stormy charge.   *Capsized by heavy swells; onset*

1360 This gudly carvel, taiklyt traist on raw,   *fast ship; rigged securely everywhere*
With blanschyt sail, mylk-quhyte as ony snaw,   *bleached*
Rycht sover tycht and wondir strangly beildyt,   *safely watertight; constructed*
Wes on the boldyn wallys quyte ovirthraw.   *swelling waves; overturned*
Contrariusly the bustuus wynd did blaw   *rough*
1365 In bubbys thik, that na schip sail mycht weld it. *heavy gusts; could cope with*
Now sank scho law, now hie tyl hevyn upheldyt.   *raised*
At every part the see and wyndis drave   *buffeted*
Quhill on a sand the schip tobryst and clave.   *Until; shore; shattered and split*

It wes a pietuus thyng, allake, allake,   *dreadful; alas*
1370 Till here the duylfull cry quhen that scho strake, *mournful; went aground*
Maist lamentabill the peryst folk till se   *doomed*

---

[1] *You may perceive your wretched world to be in now*

[2] *Who perished in the tumult of the heaving waves*

	Sa famyst, drokyt, mait, forwrocht, and wake[1]	
	Sum on a plank of firre and sum of ake,	*fir; oak*
	Sum hang apon takill, sum on a tre,	*rigging; spar*
1375	Sum fra thair gryp sone weschyne with the se.	*quickly washed away*
	Part drynt, and part to the rolke flet or swam,	*Some drowned; rock floated*
	On rapis or burdis, syne up the hill thay clam.	*ropes; planks then; climbed*

	Tho at my Nynphe breifly I did inquere	*Then; ask*
	Quhat sygnyfyit tha feirfull wondris fere.	*that set of frightening portents*
1380	"Yone multitude," said scho, "of pepill drint	
	Ar faythles folk, quhilkis, quhyle thay ar here,	*while they are alive*
	Mysknawys God, and followys thare plesere,	*Refuse to acknowledge God*
	Quhairfore thay sall in endles fyre be brynt.	*For which reason; burnt*
	Yone lusty schip thow seyst peryst and tynt,	*saw wrecked and lost*
1385	In quhame yone pepill maid ane parralus race,	*In which; perilous voyage*
	Scho heycht the Carvell of the State of Grace.	*is named*

	"Ye bene all borne the sonnys of ire I ges,	*anger; reckon*
	Syne throw baptyme gettis grace and faythfulnes.	*baptism*
	Than in yone carvell suyrly ye remane,	*safely*
1390	Oft stormstad with this warldis brukkyllnes	*storm-stayed; this world's instability*
	Quhill that ye fall in synne and wrachitnes.	*Until; degradation*
	Than, schipbrokyn, sall ye droun in endles pane,	*shipwrecked; drown*
	Except bye fayth ye fynd the plank agane,	
	Bye Chryst, workyng gud workys, I onderstand.	*With Christ's help*
1395	Remane thair with; thir sall you bryng to land.	*this (plank)*

	"This may suffice," said scho, "twychand this part.	*concerning*
	Returne thy hed, behald this othir art,	*Turn; region*
	Considdir wondris, and be vigilant	*See marvellous things*
	That thow may bettir endytyng eftirwart	*the better write afterwards*
1400	Thyngis quhilkis I sall the schaw or we depart.	*which I shall show you before*
	Thow sall have fouth of sentence and not skant.	*wealth of eloquence; scarcity*
	Thare is no welth nor welfare thow sall want.	*prosperity; lack*
	The gret Palyce of Honour salt thou se.	
	Lift up thy hed. Behald that sicht," quod sche.	

---

[1] *So starving, drenched, exhausted (checkmated), overcome with toil, and weak*

1405	At hir commaund I rasit hie on hycht high	*aloft*
	My vissage till behald that hevenly sycht.	*My face to*
	Bot tyl discryve this matter in effek	*describe; successfully*
	Impossibill wer till ony erdly wicht.	*for any mortal person*
	It transcendes sa far abone my micht	*above my powers*
1410	That I with ynk may do bot paper blek.	*may only make the paper black*
	I man draw furth, the yok lyis in my nek	*I must pull onwards; yoke; upon*
	As of the place to say my lewd avyse.	*ignorant opinion*
	Plenyst with plesance, lyke to parradyce,	*Replenished with delightful things*
	I saw a plane of peirles pulcritude	*level tract of matchless beauty*
1415	Quharein abondyt every thingis gude:	*Upon which abounded all good things*
	Spyce, wyne, corn, ule, tre, frute, flour, herbis grene,	*olive oil*
	All foulys, bestis, byrdys and alkynde fude.	*all kinds of food*
	All maner fyschis, bayth of see and flude,	*river*
	Wer kepit in pondis of polist silver schene	*polished; bright*
1420	With purifyit wattir as of the cristall clene.	*as if made from crystal*
	Till noy the small the grete bestis had na will	*attack; beasts; desire*
	Nor ravanus fowlys the littil volatill.	*predatory; little birds*
	Styll in the season all thyng remanyt thare	*Always in season; lasted*
	Perpetually, but othir noy or fare.	*without either trouble or conflict*
1425	Ay rypyt were bayth herbys, frute and flouris.	*Always ripened*
	Of every thyng the namys till declare	
	Until my febill wyt impossybill ware.	*For; it would be impossible*
	Amyd the med replete of swete odouris,	*meadow; filled with*
	A palyce stude with mony riall touris	*magnificent towers*
1430	Quhare kernellys quent, feil turretis men mycht fynd	*intricate battlements, many*
	And goldyn fanys wavand with the wynd.	*banners waving*
	Pynnakillis, fyellis, tournpikes mony one,	*Pinnacles, finials, spiral staircases*
	Gylt byrnyst torris, quhilk lyk til Phebus schone,	*Gilded [and] polished knobs*
	Skarsement, repryse, corbell, and battelyngis,[1]	
1435	Fulyery, borduris of mony pretius stone,	*Ornamental leaf patterns*
	Suttyl muldry wrocht mony day agone	*Fancy moulding*
	On buttres, jalmys, pilleris and plesand spryngis,	*door-jambs; bases for arches*

---

[1] *Wall-recess(es), indented mouldings, projecting stone brace(s), and battlements*

	Quyke ymagry with mony lusty syngis	*Lifelike carvings; effigies*
	Thare mycht be sene, and mony worthy wychtis	
1440	Tofore the yet, arrayit all at rychtis.	*In front of the gate; properly*

Furth past my Nymphe; I followyt subsequent. *passed; after*
Straucht throw the plane to the first ward we went *across; guarded entrance*
Of the palyce and entryt at that port. *gateway*
Thare saw we mony statelie tornament,
1445 Lancis brokyn, knychtis layd on the bent. *knocked to the ground*
Plesand pastance and mony lusty sport *pastime*
Thair saw we als, and sum tyme battel mort. *mortal combat*
"All thir," quod scho, "on Venus service wakis *these people; engage*
In dedis of armys for thayr ladyis sakis."

1450 Vissyand I stude the principal place but pere, *I stood gazing at; without equal*
That hevynly palyce, all of crystall clere, *all made of*
Wrocht, as me thocht, of polyst beriall stone. *Made; polished beryl*
Bosiliall nor Oliab, but were, *Bezaleel; Aholiab; without doubt*
Quhilk Sancta Sanctorum maid, maist ryche and dere, *The Holy of Holies*
1455 Nor he that wrocht the tempill of Salomon, *constructed; Solomon*
Nor he that beild the riall Ylyon, *built; Ilion*
Nor he that forgete Darius sepulture *forged the sepulchre of Darius*
Couth not performe sa craftely a cure. *Could; so ingenious a task*

Studiand here on, my Nimphe on to me spak: *While I was looking intently*
1460 "Thus in a stare quhy standis thou stupefak, *stupefied*
Gouand all day and na thyng hes vissyte! *Gaping; haven't been to see anything*
Thow art prolixt. In haist retourn thy bak. *long-winded; haste turn around*
Go efter me, and gud attendence tak. *pay close attention*
Quhat thow seyst, luke eftirwartis thow write. *Whatever you see, make sure*
1465 Thow sall behald all Venus blys perfyte." *behold; perfect joy*
Thairwith sche till ane garth did me convoy *to an enclosed garden guided me*
Quhare that I saw eneuche of perfyte joy. *plenty of*

Amyd a trone with stonys ryche ovirfret *throne; overspread*
And claith of gold, lady Venus wes set. *seated*
1470 By hir, hir sonne Cupyd quhilk nathing seys. *who sees nothing*
Quhare Mars entrit, na knawlege mycht I get. *had entered*
Bot straucht afore Venus vissage but let *directly before; face without obstacle*

Twelf amarant stagis stude, twelf grene precius greis,	*emerald steps; levels*
Quhareon thare grew thre curius goldyn treis	*stood three finely wrought posts*
1475 Sustenttand weil, the goddis face aforne,	*Carrying; before*
A fair myrrour, be thaym quently upborn.	*ingeniously supported*
Quhare of it makyt wes I have na feil —	*Of what substance; no knowledge*
Of beriall, cristall, glas or byrnyst steil,	*polished steel*
Of diamant or of the carbunkill jem:	*carbuncle gem*
1480 Quhat thing it wes diffyne may I not weil.	*I cannot properly specify*
Bot all the bordure circulare, every deill,	*circular border; part*
Wes plate of gold, — cais, stok and uthir hem —	*frame, support and outer edge*
With vertuus stanis picht that blud wald stem.	*inset; stop the flow of blood*
For quha that wound wes in the tornament	*whoever; wounded*
1485 Wox hale fra he apon the myrrour blent.	*Became unhurt after; glanced*
This riall rillik, so ryche and radius,	*magnificent relic; radiant*
Sa pollyst, plesand, purifyed, precius,	*polished*
Quhoys bontyis half to wryt I not presume,	*The half of whose virtues*
Thairon tyll se wes sa dellicius	*delightful*
1490 And sa excelland schadois gratius,	*such; reflections*
Surmontyng far in brichtnes, to my dome,	*Surpassing; in my opinion*
The costly subtil quent spectacle of Rome	*ingenious, elaborate mirror*
Or yet the myrrour send to Canyce	*sent; Canace*
Quhairin men micht ful many wondrys se.	*very many*
1495 In that myrrour I mycht se at a sycht	*see; glance*
The dedes and fetes of every erdly wycht,	*feats; mortal person*
All thinges gone lyk as they wer present,	*as if*
All the creacion of the angeilys brycht,	*angels*
Of Lucifer the fall for all his mycht,	*the fall of Lucifer despite*
1500 Adam fyrst maid and in the erth ysent.	*created; placed upon the earth*
And Noys flude thair saw I subsequent,	*Noah's Flood; after*
Babilon beild, that toure of sic renoun,	*Babel built; tower; such fame*
Of Sodomus the fele subversyoun.	*Sodom; great overthrow*
Abram, Ysak, Jacob, Josoph I saw,	*Isaac*
1505 Hornyt Moyses with his ald Ebrew law,	*Hebrew (see note)*
Twelf plagis in Egypt sent for thair trespas,	*plagues; sin*
In the Reid See with al hys court on raw	*Red Sea; together*

Kyng Pharo drynt that God wald nevir knaw — *never acknowledge God*
I saw quhat wyse the see devydyt was *in what way; sea*
1510 And all the Ebrewes dry fut ovir it pas — *Hebrews; dry-shod*
Syne in desert I saw thaym fourty yeris. *Afterwards*
Of Josuy I saw the worthy weris. *Joshua; wars*

In Judicum the batellis strang anone *the Book of Judges*
I saw of Jepty and of Gedione, *Jephthah; Gideon*
1515 Of Ameleth the cruel homosyd, *Abimelech; murder*
The wonderful werkis of douchty duke Sampsone, *heroic*
Quhilk slew a thousand with ane assys bone, *donkey's jaw-bone*
Rent templis doun and yettis in his pryde, *Broke; gates*
Of quhais strenth mervalys this warld so wyde. *whose*
1520 I saw duke Sangor there, with many a knok *Shamgar; [who] with; blow*
Sax hundreth men slew with a plewchis sok. *Six hundred; ploughshare*

The praphet Samuell saw I in that glas
Anoynt Kyng Saule, quhais sonne Jonathas *whose*
I saw wyncus ane gret ost hym allane, *vanquish; army; by himself*
1525 Yong David sla the grysly Golyas, *Goliath*
Quhais speirheid wecht thre hundreth uncis was, *The weight of whose spearhead*
Jesbedonab the giant mekill of mane *Ishbibenob; great of strength*
Lay be the handis of douchty Davyd slane — *heroic*
With fyngris sax on athir hand but weir. *six; either; without doubt*
1530 David I saw sla baith lyon and beir. *slay; bear*

This David, eik, at ane onset astond *also; surprised by an attack*
Aucht hundreth men I saw hym bryng to grond. *Eight*
With hym I saw Bananyas the strang *Benaiah*
Quhilk twa lyonys of Moab did confond *Who; overcome*
1535 And gave the stalwart Ethiop dedis wond *Ethiopian; a mortal wound*
With his awyn spere that of his hand he thrang. *i.e., the Ethiopian's own; threw*
Onabysytly this champion saw I gang *Dauntlessly; walk*
In a deip sistern and thare a lyon slewch *Into; cistern; slew*
Quhilk in a storme of snaw did harm eneuch. *snow-storm; plenty of damage*

1540 Of Salomon, the wysdom and estate, *Solomon; high dignity*
Thare saw I, and his ryche tempill, God wate, *knows*
His sonne Roboam, quhilk throw his hely pride *Rehoboam; presumptuous*

	Tynt all his ligis hartis be his fate —	*Alienated; lieges'*
	He wes to thaym sa outragius ingrate	*so flagrantly ungrateful [that]*
1545	Of twelf tribis, ten did fra hym devyd.	*the Twelve Tribes of Israel*
	I saw the angell sla, be nychtis tyd,	*slay at night-time*
	Four score thousandis of Synachorybis ost	*Sennacherib's army*
	Quhilkis come to weir on Jowry with gret bost.	*Who came; Judea; threatening*

	I saw the lyfe of the kyng Esachy	*Hezekiah*
1550	Prolongit fifteen yere, and the prophet Hely	*Elijah*
	Amyd a fyry chare to Paradyce went;	*Upon; chariot*
	The stories of Esdras and of Neamy	*Nehemiah*
	And Danyell in the lyonys cave saw I	
	For he the dragon slew, Bell brak and schent,	*Baal [he] broke and shamed*
1555	The chyldir thre amyd the fornace sent.[1]	
	I saw the transmygracion in Babillon	*deportation of the Jews to Babylon*
	And baith the bukis of Parelipomenon.	*both; Chronicles*

	I saw the haly archangell Raphell	*holy; Raphael*
	Mary Sara the dochter of Raguell	*Marry; daughter*
1560	On Thobyas for his just fatheris sake,	*To Tobias*
	And bynd the crewel devyll that wes sa fel	*cruel devil (Asmodeus); fierce*
	Quhilk slew hir sevin first husbandis, as tha tel,	*Who; as they say*
	And quhow Judyth Olyfarnus heid of strake	*Holofernes' head cut off*
	Be nychtis tyd, and fred hir town fra wrake.	*freed; from destruction*
1565	Jonas in the quhalys wame dais thre	*whale's belly three days*
	And schot furth syne, I saw, at Ninive.	*vomited forth afterwards; Nineveh*

	Of Job I saw the patyence maist degest.	*most firm*
	Of Alexander I saw the gret conquest,	
	Quhilk in twelf yeris wan nere the warld on breid,	*Who; almost the whole world*
1570	And of Anthiacus the gret onrest,	*caused by Antiochus; turmoil*
	Quhow tyrrand-lyk all Jowrye he opprest;	*tyrannically; Judea; oppressed*
	Of Macabeus, full mony knychtly deid,	*Judas Maccabeus*
	That gart all Grece and Egypt stand in dreid,	*caused; to become afraid of him*
	In quyet brocht his realm throw his prowes.	*Returned to peacefulness*
1575	I saw his brethir Symon and Jonathas,	*brothers Simon and Jonathan*

---

[1] *[I saw] the three young men (Shadrach, Meschach, and Abednego) sent into the furnace*

Quhilkis wer maist worthy quhil thair dayis rang.	*Who; during their lifetimes*
Of Tebes, eik, I saw the weris lang	*Thebes also; long wars*
Quhare Thedeus allone slew fyfty knychtis,	*Where Tideus single-handed*
Quhow fynaly of Grece the campyonys strang —	*champions*
1580 All hail the floure of knychtheid — in that thrang	*All of the very best; tumult*
Wes distroyit, quhill Thesyus with his mychtis	*until Theseus*
The toun and Creon wan, for all his slychtis.	*overcame; his (Creon's) wiles*
Thare saw I quhow, as Stacius dois tell,	*how; Statius*
Amphiorax the bischop sank to Hel.	
1585 The faithfull ladyis of Grece I mycht considdir	*could view*
In clathis blak all barfute pas togyddir	
Till Thebes sege fra thair lordis wer slane:	*To; after*
Behald, ye men that callys ladyis liddir	*wicked*
And lycht of latis, quhat kyndnes brocht thaym thidder,	*fickle in behavior*
1590 Quhat treuth and luif did in thair brestis remane.	*loyalty; reside*
I traist ye sall reid in na wryt agane	*in no other book*
In a realme sa mony of sic constance.	*one realm*
Persave thairby wemen ar til avance.	*Recognize; are to be praised*
Of duke Pyrrotheus the spousage in that tyd	*Pirithous; wedding; time*
1595 Quhare the Centauris reft away the bryd	*carried off the bride*
Thare saw I, and thair battell huge till se,	
And Hercules, quhais renoun walkis wyd,	*whose fame is widespread*
For Exiona, law by Troyis syd,	*Hesione, down by the walls of Troy*
Fecht and ovircome a monsture of the se,	*Fought; sea*
1600 For quhilk, quhen his reward denyit wes, he	*which*
Maid the first sege and the distructioun	
Of mychty Troy, quhylum the rial town.	*once; royal*
To wyn the fleys of gold tho saw I sent	*fleece; then*
Of Grece the nobillis with Jason consequent,	*From; accompanying*
1605 Hail that conquest and all Medeas slychtis,	*That whole; wiles*
Quhow for Jason Ysiphile wes schent,	*Hypsipyle; shamed*
And quhow to Troy, as thay to Colchos went,	
Grekis tholyt of kyng Lamedon gret onrychtis,	*suffered; Laomedon; injustices*
Quhairfore Troy distroyt wes be thair mychtis,	*For which reason*
1610 Exiona ravyst and Lamedon slane,	*Hesione abducted*
Bot Priamus restoryt the town agane.	*rebuilt*

	The Jugement of Parys saw I syne	*then*
	That gave the appil (as poetis can diffyne)	*as poets state*
	Till Venus as goddes maist gudlye,	*most beautiful*
1615	And quhow in Grece he revest quene Helyne	*abducted*
	Quharefore the Grekis with thair gret navyn,	*naval force*
	Full mony thousand knychtis, hastely	
	Thaym till revenge salyt towart Troy in hye.	*sailed; in haste*
	I saw quhow be Ulixes with gret joy	*how by Ulysses*
1620	Quhat wyse Achil wes fond and brocht to Troy.	*By what means; found; brought*

	The crewel battellys and the dyntis strang,	*fierce attacks*
	The gret debate, and eik the weris lang	*strife; also*
	At Troy sege, the myrrour to me schew,	*siege*
	Sustenit ten yeris, Grekis Troianys amang,	*Trojans surrounded by Greeks*
1625	And athir party set ful oft in thrang,	*either; into the tumult*
	Quhare that Hector did douchty dedis enew,	*plenty of brave deeds*
	Quhilk fears Achil (baith hym and Troylus) slew.	*Whom fierce*
	The gret hors maid I saw, and Troy syn tynt	*Trojan Horse; lost*
	And fair Ylion al in flambys brynt.	*Ilion; flames burnt*

1630	Syne out of Troy I saw the fugityvys,	*Then*
	Quhow that Eneas, as Virgill weil discrivis,	*Aeneas*
	In countries seir wes by the seis rage	*To; many; the sea's fury*
	Bewavyt oft, and quhow that he arryvys	*Driven repeatedly; how*
	With all his flote but danger of theyr lyvys,	*fleet without*
1635	And quhow thay wer reset, baith man and page,	*sheltered both old and young*
	Be quene Dido, remanand in Cartage,	*By; staying*
	And quhow Eneas syne (as that they tell)	*then*
	Went for to seik his father doun in Hell.	*seek*

	Ovir Stix the flude I saw Eneas fair,	*the River Styx; go*
1640	Quhare Carone wes the bustuus feryair.	*Charon; the churlish ferryman*
	The fludis four of Hell thair mycht I se,	*rivers; could*
	The folk in pane, the wayis circulair,	*pain; paths*
	The weltrand stone wirk Sisipho mych cair	*rolling; cause Sisyphus much trouble*
	And all the plesance of the Camp Elysee	*delight; Elysian Fields*
1645	Quhare ald Anchyses did common with Enee,	*converse*
	And schew be lyne all his successyon.	*showed by lineal descent; progeny*
	This ilk Eneas, maist famus of renoun,	

I saw to goddis make the sacrifice
(Quhairof the ordour and maner to devys   *Of which; sequence; set forth*
1650   Wer ovir prolext), and quhow Eneas syne   *too lengthy; how; then*
Went to the schyp, and eik I saw quhat wyse   *in what way*
All his navy gret hunger did suppryse,   *hunger overtook all his navy*
Quhow he in Italie fynalie, with huge pyne,   *great suffering*
Arrivit at the strandis of Lavyne,   *shores*
1655   And quhow he faucht weil, baith on land and seys,   *fought*
And Tarnus slew, the kyng of Rutuleis.   *Turnus; Rutulians*

Rome saw I beildit fyrst be Romulus,   *first built*
And eik quhow lang (as wryttis Levius)   *also; Livy*
The Romane kyngis abone the pepill rang,   *reigned over the people*
1660   And how the wickit proud Terquinius,   *Tarquin*
With wyfe and barnis, be Brutus Junius   *children*
Wer exilit Rome for thair insufferabil wrang.
Bot al the proces for to schaw wer lang,   *to tell the whole tale*
Quhow chast Lucres, the gudliest and best,   *Lucrece*
1665   Be Sextus Terquine wes cruelly opprest.   *raped*

The Punik batalis in that mirrour cleir   *Punic Wars*
Atwene Cartage and Romanis mony yeir   *Between Carthage and Rome*
I saw — becaus Eneas pietuus   *god-fearing Aeneas*
Fled fra Dido be admonicionis seir.   *because of many admonitions*
1670   Atwene thair pepil rais ane langsum weir.   *Between; long-lasting*
I saw quhow worthy Marcus Regulus
Maist valiant, prudent and victorius
Howbeit he micht at liberty gone fre   *Even though*
For common profyt chesyt for till de.   *For the good of the community; die*

1675   Tullus Servilius, dowchty in his daw,   *Tullius Servius, valiant in his day*
And Marcus Curtius eik in the myrrour I saw,   *also*
Quhilk, throw his stowtenes, in the fyry gap   *courage into the fiery crevice*
For common profyt of Rome him self did thraw   *welfare; threw himself*
Richt onabasitly, havand na dreid nor aw: *Utterly unafraid*
1680   Montit on hors, onarmyt, thairin lap.   *fully armed; leapt*
And Hannyball I saw, by fatell hap   *fated occurrence*
Wyn contrare Romanys mony fair victory   *against*
Quhyll Scipio eclypsyt all hys glory.   *Scipio Africanus overshadowed*

	This worthy Scipio clepyt Affrycane	*called*
1685	I saw vincus thys Hannyball in plane	*vanquish; in the field*
	And Cartage bryng untyll fynall rewyn	*ruin*
	And to Rome conquerit all the realme of Spane.	
	Quhow Kyng Jugurtha hes his brethir slane	*brothers*
	Thare saw I eik, and of his were the fyne.	*also; war; conclusion*
1690	Rycht weil I saw the batellis intestyne	*civil war*
	Of Catulyna and of Lentulus	*Lucius Catiline*
	And atwine Pompey and Cesar Julyus,	*between Pompey the Great; Julius Caesar*

	And, breifly, every famus douchty deid	*courageous act*
	That men in story may se or cornakyll reid.	*chronicle*
1695	I mycht behald in that myrrour expres	*precisely*
	The miserie, the crewelte, the dreid,	
	Pane, sorow, wo, baith wretchitnes and neid,	
	The gret envy, covatus, dowbilnes	*greed; treachery*
	Twychand warldly onfaithful brukkylnes[1]	
1700	I saw the Fend fast folk to vicis tist	*Devil; entice*
	And al the cumming of the Antecrist.	*Antichrist*

	Plesand debaitmentis, quha sa rycht reportis,	*Pleasant discussions*
	Thare mycht be sene and al maner disportys:	*recreations*
	The falkonnis for the revere at thair gate	*falcons to the river; ambush*
1705	Newand the fowlys in periculo mortis[2]	
	Layand thaym in be companeis and sortis[3]	
	(And, at the plunge, part saw I handlyt hate!);[4]	
	The wery huntare, byssy ayr and late,	*weary; busy early*
	Wyth questyng hundis syrchand to and fra	*[I saw] searching*
1710	To hunt the hart, the bare, the da, the ra.	*boar; doe; roe-deer*

	I saw Raf Coilyear with his thrawin brow,	*frowning*
	Craibit Johne the reif and auld Cowkewyis sow	*Irritable; reeve; old*
	And how the wran come out of Ailssay,	*wren; Ailsa Crag*

---

[1] *Involved in the treacherous instability of the world*

[2] *Chasing the birds, in danger of death, into the water*

[3] *Enclosing them according to their flocks and species*

[4] *And, during their dive underwater, I saw some (of the birds) treated harshly*

	And Peirs Plewman that maid his workmen fow,	*Piers Plowman; made; well-fed*
1715	Gret Gowmakmorne and Fyn Makcoull, and how	*(see note)*
	Thay suld be goddis in Ireland, as thay say.	*are supposed to be*
	Thair saw I Maitland upon auld beird gray,	*old Greybeard*
	Robene Hude and Gilbert with the quhite hand,	*white*
	How Hay of Nauchtoun flew in Madin land.	*Fairyland*

1720	The nigramansy thair saw I eik anone	*conjuring*
	Of Bonitas, Bongo, and Frere Bacon	*(see note)*
	With mony subtell poynt of juglory:	*cunning trick of jugglery*
	Of Flandris peys maid mony precius stone,	*From Flanders peas*
	A gret lade sadil of a sychyng bone,	*pack-saddle; funny bone?*
1725	Of a nutmog thay mayid a monk in hy,	*nutmeg; haste*
	A parys kirk of a small penny py,	*parish church; pie*
	And Bonytas of a mussil made ane ape,	*mussel*
	With mony othir subtell mow and jape.	*cunning jest and trick*

	And schortly, til declare the veryte,	*to tell the truth in brief*
1730	All plesand pastance and gemmys that micht be	*pastime; games*
	In that myrrour wer present to my sycht.	
	And as I wondryt on that grete ferlye,	*marvel*
	Venus at last, in turning of hir e,	*eye*
	Knew weil my face and said, "Be Goddis micht,	
1735	Ye bene welcum, my presoner, to this hycht.	*height*
	Quhow passit thou," quod scho, "that hidduus depe?"	
	"Madame," quod I, "I not more than a schepe."	*know no more; sheep*

	"Na fors thairof," said scho, "sen thow art here.	*That is not important; since*
	Quhow plesys the our pastance and effere?"	*pleases; performance*
1740	"Glaidly," quod I, "Madame, be God of hevyn."	
	"Remembris thow," said scho, "withouten were,	*doubt*
	On thy promyt quhen of thy gret dangere	*promise; when from*
	I the deliverit (as now is not to nevyn)?"	*which; mention*
	Than answerit I agane with sober stevyn:	*dignified voice*
1745	"Madame, your precept, quhat so be your wyll,	*whatever is*
	Here I remane ay reddy till fulfill."	

| | "Weil, weil," said scho, "thy wyll is suffycyent. | |
| | Of thy bousoum answere I stand content." | *humble* |

1750	Than suddandly in hand a buke scho hynt	*took hold of*
	The quhilk to me betaucht scho or I went,	*Which she entrusted to me; before*
	Commandand me to be obedient	
	And put in ryme that proces than quyt tynt.	*narrative; quite forgotten*
	I promised hir, forsuyth, or scho wald stynt,	*indeed; before she finished*
	The buke ressavand, thairon my cure to preve.	*receiving; diligence; test*
1755	Inclynand syne lawly, I tuke my leve.	*Bowing; humbly; leave*

	Twychand this buke peraventur ye sall here	*Concerning; perhaps; hear*
	Sumtyme efter quhen I have mare lasere.	*more leisure*
	My Nymphe in hast tho hynt me by the hand	*took*
	And as we sammyn walkyt furth in fere	*together; side by side*
1760	"I the declare," sayd scho, "yone myrrour clere	*explain to you [that]*
	The quhilk thow saw afore dame Venus stand	
	Signifyes nothing ellis till understand	*else*
	Bot the gret bewty of thir ladyis facis	
	Quhairin lovers thinkis thay behald all gracis."	*In which; perceive*

1765	Scho me convoyit, finally to tell,	*took me*
	With gret plesance straucht to the ryche castell,	*straight*
	Quhare mony saw I pres til get ingres.	*entrance*
	Thare saw I Synon and Achittefell	*Ahithophel*
	Pressand til clym the wallis and how thay fell.	*Pushing forward*
1770	Lucyus Catalyn saw I thare expres,	*clearly*
	In at a wyndow pres til have entres	*push; entry*
	Bot suddandly Tullius come with a buke,	*Marcus Tullius Cicero*
	And strake hym doun quhill all his chaftis quuke.	*struck; until; jaws shook*

	Fast clymmand up thay lusty wallys of stone	*those*
1775	I saw Jugurtha and tressonabill Tryphon	
	Bot thay na grippis thair mycht hald for slyddir.[1]	
	Preissand to clym stude thousandis many one,	*Pushing forward*
	And into the ground thay fallen every one.	
	Than on the wall a garatour I considdir,	*tower watchman; looked at*
1780	Proclamand lowd, that did thayr hartis swiddir:	*who made their hearts falter*
	"Out on falshed, the mother of everye vyce!	*Down with*

---

[1] *But they couldn't find any foothold because of the slipperiness (of that wall)*

Away invy and brynnand covetyce!" *burning covetousness*

The garatour, my Nymphe tho to me tald, *explained*
Wes clepyt Lawte, kepar of the hald *Loyalty, keeper; stronghold*
1785 Of hie honour, and thay pepyll out schete *those; shut out*
Swa presand thaym to clym, quilum wer bald,[1]
Rycht vertuus young; but fra tyme thay woux ald, *once they grew old*
Fra honour hail one vice thair mindis sete. *wholly on to*
"Now sall thow go," quod sche, "straucht to the yete, *gate*
1790 Of this palyce and entre but offence, *without*
For the portar is clyped Pacience. *doorkeeper*

"The mychty prynce, the gretest Empriour
Of yone palyce," quod scho, "hecht hie Honour, *is named*
Quham to disservys mony traist officiare. *Who is served by; trusted*
1795 For Charité, of gudlynes the flour, *the paragon*
Is Maister Houshald in yone cristall tour, *Master of the Household; that*
Ferme Constance is the kyngis secritare *Loyal; secretary*
And Liberalite heicht his thesaurar. *is the name of; treasurer*
Innocens and Devocyon, as efferis, *as is fitting*
1800 Bene clerkis of closet and cubeculeris.[2]

"His Comptrowere is clepyt Discretioun. *Comptroller (revenues officer)*
Humanyte and Trew Relatioun *Courtesy; Fair Report*
Bene yscherris of his chalmer morow and eve. *ushers; chamber*
Peace, Quyet, Rest, oft wakis up and doun *regularly walk*
1805 In till his hall as marchellis of renoun. *hall-marshals; renown*
Temperance is cuke, his mete to tast and preve. *cook; taste and test*
Humylyté, karvar, that na wycht lyst greve. *carver; wishes to offend no one*
His maister sewer hecht Vertuus Discipline. *waiter is named*
Mercy is copper, and mixis weil his wyne. *cup-bearer*

1810 "His chanceller is clepyt Conscyence, *law officer; named*
Quhilk for na meid will pronounce fals sentence. *Who; no bribe*
With him are assessouris four of one ascent, *deputies; of one accord*

---

[1] *Thus urging themselves forward to climb [who] once were bold [and]*
[2] *Are royal confessors and attendants of the royal bedchamber*

Science, Prudence, Justice, Sapience, — *Knowledge; Wisdom*
Quhilkis to na wycht lyst committing offence[1]
1815 The chekker rollys and the kyngis rent — *exchequer account books; income*
As auditouris thay ovirseis quhat is spent.
Labourus Diligens, Gud Werkis, Clene Livyng
Bene out-stewartis and catouris to yone kyng.[2]

"Gud Hope remanys ever amang yone sort, — *stays always; that company*
1820 A fyne menstral with mony mow and sport. — *jest and joke*
And Pieté is the kyngis almoseir. — *almoner (distributor of alms)*
Syne Fortitude (the rycht quha lyst report) — *whoever wishes to describe aright*
Is lieutenand, al wrachys to comfort. — *royal deputy; destitute people*
The kyngis mynyeon, roundand in his eyr — *confidant, whispering*
1825 Heicht Verite, did nevir leyl man deir,[3]
And, schortly, every vertew and plesance — *in summary*
Is subject to yone kyngis obbeysance. — *bound in obedience to that king*

"Come on," sayd sche, "this ordenance to vysyte." — *establishment*
Than past we to that cristall palyce quhyte — *white*
1830 Quhare I abayd the entre til behald. — *Where; lingered; look at*
I bad na mare of plesance nor delyte, — *could expect nothing greater*
Of lusty sycht, of joy and blys perfyte,
Nor mare weilfare til have abone the mold, — *good fortune; upon the earth*
Than for til se that yet of byrnyst gold, — *gate of burnished*
1835 Quhare on thair was maist curiusly ingrave — *Upon which; skilfully engraved*
All naturall thyng men may in erd consave. — *in the world imagine*

Thare wes the erth enveronyt wyth the see — *surrounded by*
Quhare on the schyppes saland mycht I se, — *Upon which; sailing*
The ayr, the fyre — all the four elymentis —
1840 The Speris Sevyn and Primum Mobile, — *Spheres; outermost sphere*
The Sygnis Twelf, perfytly every gre, — *twelve astrological signs; degree*
The Zodiak, hale as bukis represents, — *exactly*
The Poil Antertik that ever himselfe absentis, — *(see note)*

---

[1] *Who do not wish to commit a breach of law against anyone*

[2] *Are administrators of outlying regions and buyers of provisions for the king*

[3] *Is named Truth, (who) never injured a loyal man*

The Poil Artik, and eik the Ursis twane,   *also Ursa Major and Ursa Minor*
1845 The Sevyn Sterris, Pheton and the Charle Wane.   *(see note)*

Thare wes ingraf quhow that Ganamedis   *engraved; Ganymede*
Wes reft till hevyn (as men in Ovyd redis),   *abducted*
And on till Jupiter made his cheif butlare;
The douchters, fare in to thayr lusty wedis,   *attractive in their fine clothes*
1850 Of Dorida, amyd the see but dredis   *Driada; without doubt*
Swymmand, and part wer figurit thare   *depicted*
Apon a crag dryand thair yalow hare —   *hair*
With facis not onlyk, for quha thaym seyng   *so that whoever saw them*
Mycht weil consyddir that thay al sisteris beyng.   *readily perceive; were*

1855 Of the planetis all the conjunctionys,   *conjunctions (see note)*
Thare episciclis and opposionis   *epicycles; oppositions*
Wer porturyt thair, and quhow thair coursis swagis,   *depicted; movement decreases*
Thare naturale and dayly motionis,   *natural; daily*
Eclipse, aspectis and degressyonys.   *relative positions; deviations from course*
1860 Thare saw I mony gudly personagis   *portraits*
Quhilkis semyt all lusty quyk ymagis,   *Which seemed; lifelike*
The werkmanschip excedyng mony fold   *many times*
The precyus mater, thocht it wes fynest gold.   *even though*

Wondrand here on, agane my wyll but lete   *without hesitation*
1865 My Nymphe in grif schot me in at the yet.   *in anger; pushed; gate*
"Quhat devyl," said scho, "hes thou not ellis ado   *have you nothing else to do*
Bot all thy wyt and fantasy to set   *intelligence and perceptiveness*
On sic dotyng?" and tho for fere I swet   *folly; sweated*
Of her langage, bot than anone said scho,   *Because of; soon*
1870 "List thou se farlyes, behald thaym yondir, lo;   *If you want to see marvels*
Yit study not ovir mekil a dreid thow vary,[1]
For I persave the halflyngis in a fary."   *halfway into a trance*

Within that palyce sone I gat a sycht   *soon*
Quhare walkand went ful mony worthy wicht
1875 Amyd the close, with all myrthys to wale;   *courtyard; pleasures to choose from*

---

[1] *But do not inspect too closely lest you go insane*

The Palis of Honoure

For lyk Phebus with fyry bemys brycht
The wallys schane, castand sa gret a lycht,   *shone*
It semyt lyk the hevyn imperiall.   *empyrean (the highest heavens)*
And as the cedir surmontyth the rammale   *cedar overtops the brushwood*
1880 In perfyt hycht, sa of that court a glance
Excedis far all erdly vane plesance.

For lois of sycht considdir micht I nocht   *loss; I could not reckon*
Quhow perfytly the ryche wallys wer wrocht.   *constructed*
Swa the reflex of cristall stanys schone,   *The reflection from; shone so*
1885 For brychtnes skarsly blenk thairon I mocht[1]
The purifyit silver (soithly as me thocht)   *refined; (as it certainly seemed to me)*
Insteid of syment wes ovir all that wone,   *In place of mortar; dwelling*
Yet round about ful mony a beriall stone,   *Poured*
And thaym conjunctly jonyt fast and quemyt.   *joined; fitted closely*
1890 The close wes paithit with silver, as it semyt.   *courtyard; paved*

The durris and the wyndois all wer breddyt   *doors; windows; plated*
With massy gold, quhareof the fynes scheddit.[2]
With byrnyst evyr baith palyce and touris   *polished ivory*
Wer thekyt weil, maist craftely that cled it: *roofed; covered*
1895 For so the quhitly blanchit bone ovirspred it,   *bleached-white bone*
Mydlyt with gold, anamalyt all colouris,   *Interspersed; enamelled in*
Inporturat of byrdis and swete flouris,   *Portrayed with*
Curius knottis and mony sle devyse,   *Intricate; artful design*
Quhilkis to behald wes perfyt paradice.   *to see*

1900 And, to proceid, my Nympe and I furth went   *to continue*
Straucht to the hall, throw out the palyce jent,   *Directly; straight through; noble*
And ten stagis of thopas did ascend.   *steps; topaz*
Schit wes the dure. In at a boir I blent,   *Shut; chink I peeked*
Quhare I beheld the gladdest represent   *the most gratifying scene*
1905 That evir in erth a wrachit catywe kend.   *miserable wretch saw*
Breifly theis proces til conclude and end: *this narrative*
Me thocht the flure wes al of amatist,   *It seemed to me; amethyst*

---

[1] *I could hardly glance upon them because of their brilliance*

[2] *With solid gold, from which the purity was diffused*

71

Bot quhareof war the wallis I ne wist.[1]

The multitud of prectius stonis sere	*precious; diverse*
1910 Thairon swa schane, my febill sycht, but were,	*Upon them; shone; without doubt*
Mycht not behald thair vertuus gudlynes.	*beneficial powers (see note)*
For all the ruf (as did to me appere)	*ceiling*
Hang full of plesand lowpyt saphyrs clere.	*looped (arranged in spirals)*
Of dyamantis and rubys, as I ges,	
1915 Wer all the burdis maid, of mast riches.	*tables*
Of sardanus, of jaspe and smaragdane	*sardonyx, jasper, smaragd*
Trestis, formys and benkis wer, pollist plane.[2]	

Baith to and fro amyd the hall they went,	
Rial princis in plate and armouris quent	*intricately made*
1920 Of byrnist gold cuchit with precyus stonys.	*burnished; inset*
Intronyt sat a god armypotent,	*mighty in arms (see note)*
On quhais gloryus vissage as I blent,	*looked*
In extasy, be his brychtnes, atonys	*Into a trance; suddenly*
He smate me doun and byrsyt all my bonys.	*knocked; bruised*
1925 Thare lay I still in swoun, with cullour blaucht,	*a blanched complexion*
Quhil at the last my Nymphe up hes me kaucht.	*Until; picked me up*

Syne wyth gret pane, with womentyng and care,	*lamenting; trouble*
In hir armys scho bare me doun the stare	*she carried me downstairs*
And in the clois full softly laid me doun,	*courtyard*
1930 Held up my hede to tak the hailsum ayre	*refreshing air*
For of my lyfe scho stude in gret dispare.	*she feared greatly for my life*
Me till awalk ay wes that lady boun,	*she worked unceasingly to revive me*
Quhill, finally, out of my dedly swoun	*Until*
I swyth ovircome and up my eyne did cast.	*suddenly revived; opened up my eyes*
1935 "Be myrry, man," quod scho, "the werst is past.	

"Get up," scho said, "for schame, be na cowart.	
My hede in wed, thow hes a wyfis hart	*"I'll bet my head"*
That for a plesand sycht is so mysmaid!"	*upset*

---

[1] *But of what substance the walls were made I did not know*

[2] *Trestles, seats, and benches were, polished smooth*

Than, all in anger, apon my fete I start;   *upon my feet I sprang*
1940 And for hir wordis wer so apyrsmart,   *stinging*
On to the Nymphe I maid a bustuus braid.   *violent gesture*
"Carlyng," quod I, "quhat wes yone at thow said?" *Old woman; what was it that*
"Soft yow," said sche, "thay ar not wyse that stryvys, *Calm yourself; quarrel*
For kyrkmen wer ay jentill to ther wyvys.   *churchmen; always gentle*

1945 "I am rycht glaid thou art wordyn so wycht. *very glad; become so strong*
Lang ere (me thocht) thow had nothir fors ne mycht, *A while ago; neither*
Curage nor wyll for till have grevyt a fla. *to have bothered a flea*
Quhat alyt the to fall?" Quod I, "The sycht   *caused*
Of yone goddes grym fyry vissage brycht
1950 Ovirset my wyt and all my spretis swa   *Overcame; so that*
I mycht not stand." "Bot wes that suyth?" "Ya, ya!" *true*
Than said the Nymphe rycht merylie and leuch, *laughed*
"Now I considdir thy malt hart weil eneuch. *understand; overwhelmed; enough*

"I wyl," quod scho, "na mare the thus assay   *no more; test*
1955 With sic plesance, quhilk may thy sprete effray. *delight; frighten*
Yit sall thow se suythly (sen thou art here)   *indeed; since*
My lydyis court in thair gudly array.   *lady's*
For till behald thair myrth cum on thy way."
Than hand in hand suyth went we furth in fere *quickly; together*
1960 At a postrum towart the fair herbere.   *back door; garden*
In that passage full fast at hir I franyt   *very eagerly asked*
Quhat folk thay wer within the hall remanyt. *[who] stayed*

"Yone wer," said scho, "quha sa the richt discrivys, *whoever correctly describes*
Maist vailyeand folk and vertuus in thair lyvys. *valiant*
1965 Now in the court of Honour thay remane   *stay*
Victoriusly, and in all plesance thryvys, *Triumphantly; flourish*
For thay with spere, with swerdys and wyth knyvys
In just battell wer fundyn maist of mane. *found to be greatest of strength*
In thair promyttis thay stude evir fyrm and plane. *promises; honest*
1970 In thaym aboundit worschyp and lawte   *loyalty*
Illumynyt with liberalité.   *Made lustrous by generosity*

"Honour," quod scho "to this hevinly ryng *in this; kingdom*
Differris richt far from warldly honoring,   *Differs*

73

	Quhilk is but pompe of erdly dignyté	*Which is merely; earthly*
1975	Gyvyn for estate or blude, micht, or sic thyng.	*Awarded; rank; lineage; power*
	And in this countre, prynce, prelate or kyng	
	Alanerly sall for vertu honoryt be;	*Only*
	For erdly glore is not bot vanyte	*nothing but*
	That, as we se, sa suddandly will wend;	*very suddenly; depart*
1980	Bot vertuus honour nevir mare sall end.	*virtuous*

"Behald," said scho "and se this warldly glore:
Maist inconstant, maist slyd and transitore. *slippery*
Prosperite in erd is bot a dreme, *merely a dream*
Or lyk as man wer steppand ovir a score: *stepping over a crack*
1985 Now is he law that wes so hie tofore, *low; high before*
And he quhilum wes borne pure of his deme, *[who] once; poor; from his mother*
Now his estate schynys lyke the sonne beme. *shines*
Baith up and doun, baith to and fro we se
This warld weltrys as dois the wally see. *tumbles; rough sea*

1990 "To papis, bischoppis, prelatis and primatis, *popes*
Empriouris, kinges, princes, potestatis, *potentates*
Deth settis the terme and end of all thair hycht. *exalted state*
Fra thay be gan, late se quha on thaym watys.[1]
Na thyng remanis bot fame of thair estatis, *fame derived from their rank*
1995 And not ellis bot vertuus werkis richt *nothing else; good deeds*
Sall with thaym wend, nother thair pompe nor mycht. *depart; neither*
Ay vertu ryngis in lestand honour clere; *Eternally; reigns; lasting*
Remembir than that vertu hes no pere.

"For vertu is a thing sa precyous,
2000 Quhareof the end is sa delycious *gratifying*
The warld ma not consyddir quhat it is.
It makis folk perfyte and glorious.
It makis sanctis of pepill vicious. *saints; wicked people*
It causis folk ay leve in lestand blys. *live always*
2005 It is the way til hie honour I wys.
It dantis deth and every vice thorow mycht. *defeats*

---

[1] *Once they are gone, just see who waits on them.*

Without vertu, fy on all erdly wycht!

"Vertu is eik the perfyte sikkyr way,	*dependable*
And not ellis, til honour lestand ay.	*no other; everlasting*
2010 For mony hes sene vitious pepil upheit	*wicked people exalted*
And eftir sone thair glory vanys away,	*afterwards rapidly; vanishes*
Quharof exemplis we se this every day.	*Examples of which*
His erdly pompe is gone quhen that he deyt.	*died*
Than is he with no erdly frend suppleit	*provided*
2015 Savand vertu — weill is him hes sic a fere.	*[who] has such a companion*
Now wil I schaw," quod sche, " quhat folk bene here.	*show*

"The strangest Sampson is in to yone hald,	*building*
The forsy, pyssand Hercules so bald,	*mighty, powerful; bold*
The feirs Achill and all the Nobillis Nyne,	*fierce; Nine Worthies (see note)*
2020 Scipio Affricane, Pompeyus the ald,	
Uthir mony quhais namys afore are tald	*Many others who are named above*
With thousandis ma than I may here diffine,	*more; refer to*
And lusty ladyis amyd thay lordis syne:	*mingling with; then*
Semiramis, Thamar, Ypolytha,	*Tomyris; Hippolyta*
2025 Pantyssale, Medus, Cenobia.	*Penthesileia, Medusa, Zenobia*

"Of thy regyon yondir bene honorit part,	*Some from your land*
The kyngis Gregor, Kened and Kyng Robert,	*(see note)*
With otheris mo that beis not here rehersyt.	*more who are not named here*
Waryit," quod scho, "ay be thy megyr hart.	*Accursed; always; puny heart*
2030 Thow suld have sene, had thou biddin in yon art,	*should; stayed in that area*
Quhat wyse yone hevynly company conversyt.	*In what way; conversed*
Wa worth thy febyll brane, sa sone wes persit.	*Bad luck befall; was wounded*
Thow mycht have sene, remanand quhare thow was,	
A huge pepyl punyst for thair trespas	*great nation punished*

2035 "Quhilkis be wilfull, manyfest arrogance,	*flagrant*
Invyus pryd, pretendit ignorance,	
Fowle dowbilnes and dissate unamendit,	*trickery; unmitigated deceit*
Enforcis thaym thair selvyn til avance,	*themselves*
Be sle falsheid, but lawte or constance,	*without loyalty or constancy*
2040 Wyth subtelnes and slychtnes now commendit,	*cunning; deception; approved*
Betraisand folk that nevir to them offendit,	*Betraying*

	And upheis thaim self throw frawdful lippis,	*exalt themselves; by means of*
	Thocht God cause oft thare erdly glore eclippis.	*glory to be eclipsed*
	"And nobillis cumyn of honorabill ancestry	*descended from*
2045	Thair vertuus nobilité settis nocht by,	*do not value*
	For dishonest, unlefull, warldly ways	*Because of; disloyal*
	And throw corruppit, covatus invy.	*corrupt*
	Bot he that can be dowbill, nane is set by.	*Except for him; no one is esteemed*
	Dissate is wisdum; lawte, honour away is.	*Deceit; is gone away*
2050	Rycht few or nane takis tent thairto thir days.	*none pays heed; nowadays*
	And thair gret wrangis till reforme but let	*wrongs; without hindrance*
	In judgement yone god wes yondir set.	
	"Remanand yondir thow mycht have herd belyve	*at once*
	Pronouncit the gret sentence diffinytive	*final judgment*
2055	Twichand this actioun, and the dreidful pane	*Upon this case*
	Execute on trespassouris yit on lyve,	*now alive*
	Swa that thair malyce sall na mare prescryve."	*shall no longer hold sway*
	"Madame," quod I, "for Goddis saik, turn agane.	
	My spreit desyris to se thair torment fane."	*eagerly*
2060	Quod scho, "richt now thare sall thow be rejosyt	*right away; gratified*
	Quhen thow hes tane the ayr and bettir apposyt.[1]	
	"Bot first thow sal considdir commoditeis	*the conveniences*
	Of our gardyng, lo, full of lusty trees,	*garden*
	All hie cypres, of flewer maist fragrant.	*cypresses; odor*
2065	Our ladyis yonder, bissy as the beis,	*busy as the bees*
	The swete florist colouris of rethoreis	*ornamental devices of rhetoricians*
	Gaddris full fast, mony grene tendir plant;	*Collect very rapidly*
	For with all plesance plenist is yone hant,	*replenished; region*
	Quhare precious stanys on treis doyth abound	*stones (see note)*
2070	In sted of frute, chargyt with peirlis round."	*[they are] laden; pearls*
	On till that gudly garth thus we proceid	*To; yard*
	Quhilk with a large fowsy, fare on breid,	*ditch, broad in width*
	Inveronyt wes, quhare fysches wer enew.	*Surrounded; fishes; aplenty*

---

[1] *When you have had a breather and [are] better conditioned*

	All wattir foulis wer swomand thair gud speid;	*waterfowl; swimming [with]*
2075	Als out of growand treis thair saw I breid	*Also; breed*
	Foulys that hyngand by thair nebbis grew.	*hanging by their beaks (see note)*
	Out ovir the stank of mony divers hew	*moat of many various colours*
	Wes laid a tre, ovir quhilk behovyt we pas,	*of necessity we had to cross*
	Bot I can not declare quhare of it wes.	*of what substance*

2080	My Nymphe went ovir, chargeand me felow fast.	*ordering; follow*
	Hir till obbey my spretis woux agast,	*became terrified*
	Swa peralus wes the passagis till aspy.	*So hazardous did the path look*
	Away sche went, and fra tyme sche wes past,	*once she was across*
	Apon the bryg I entrit at the last.	*bridge*
2085	Bot swa my harnys trymlyt bissyly,	*so incessantly were my brains trembling*
	Quhyl I fell ovir and baith my fete slaid by,	*That; feet slipped past*
	Out ovir the hede, into the stank adoun,	*Head over heels into the moat below*
	Quhare, as me thocht, I wes in point to droun.	*I was about to drown*

	Quhat throw the byrdis sang and this affray,	*What with; this shock*
2090	Out of my swoun I wallkynnyt quhare I lay	*awakened*
	In the gardyn quhare I fyrst doun fell.	
	About I blent, for richt clere was the day,	*blinked*
	Bot all thys lusty plesance wes away.	
	Me thocht that fare herbere maist lyk to Hel	*garden*
2095	In till compare of this ye herd me tell.	*In comparison with; you heard me describe*
	Allace, allace. I thocht me than in pane,	
	And langyt sare for till have swounyt agane.	*longed sorely; swooned*

	The byrdis sang nor yit the mery flouris	*[Neither]; singing nor yet*
	Mycht not ameys my grevows gret dolouris.	*lessen; miseries*
2100	All erdly thyng me thocht barrant and vyle.	*sterile and loathsome*
	Thus I remanyt into the garth twa houris	*enclosed garden*
	Cursand the feildis with all the fare coullouris,	
	That I awolk oft wariand the quhyle.	*Oft cursing that I awoke so soon*
	Always my mynd wes on the lusty yle,	*isle*
2105	In purpose evir till have dwelt in that art,	*region*
	Of rethorik cullouris til have fund sum parte.	*devices of rhetoric; found*

| | And maist of all my curage wes aggrevit | *my mood was upset* |
| | Becaus sa sone I of my dreme eschevyt, | *too soon I came out of my dream* |

	Nocht seand quhow thay wrechis wer torment	*Not seeing; those wretches*
2110	That honour mankyt and honeste myschevyt.	*disfigured; honesty thwarted*
	Glaidly I wald amyd thys wryt have brevyt,	*into this book have recorded*
	Had I it sene, quhow thay were slane or schent.	*If I had seen it; humiliated*
	Bot fra I saw all thys weilfare wes went,	*once; happiness; gone*
	Till mak ane end, sittand under a tre,	*To conclude*
2115	In laude of honour I wrait thir versis thre:	*praise; wrote these three stanzas*

	"O hie honour, swete hevynly flour degest,	*dignified*
	Gem vertuus, maist precius, gudlyest	*worthiest*
	For hie renoun, thow art guerdoun condyng,	*suitable reward*
	Of worschyp kend the glorius end and rest,	*For high deeds known as*
2120	But quham, in rycht, na worthy wicht may lest;[1]	
	Thy gret puissance may maist avance all thyng,[1]	
	And poverale to myche avale sone bryng.	*poor people; great advantage*
	I the requere, sen thow, but pere, art best,	*ask thee; without rival*
	That eftir this in thy hie blys we ryng.	*reign*

2125	"Of grace thy face in every place so schynys,	*With*
	That, swete, all spreit baith heid and feit inclynis[2]	
	Thy glore afore, for til implore remeid.	*Before your glory; assistance*
	He docht rycht nocht quhilk out of thocht the tynis.[3]	
	Thy name but blame, and riall fame, dyvine is,	*without*
2130	Thow port, at schort, of our comfort and reid	*Thou; guidance*
	Tyll bryng all thyng tyll gladyng eftir deid.	*joy; after death*
	All wycht but sycht of thy gret mycht ay crinis.	*without; perpetually dwindles*
	O schene, I mene, nane may sustene thy feid.	*O brilliant one; endure; hostility*

	"Hail rois, maist chois til clois thy foys gret mycht.	*excellent to overcome; foe's*
2135	Hail stone quhilk schone apon the trone of lycht.	*throne*
	Vertew, quhais trew suet dew overthrew all vyce,	*whose; sweet dew*
	Was ay, ilk day, gar say, the way of lycht.	*always; everyday, [I] dare say*
	Amend offend, and send our end ay richt.	*offence; always right*

---

[1] *2120-21: Without which, as is just, no worthy person can continue;*
   Thy great power can bring the most advancement to all things

[2] *That, sweetly, every spirit (person) inclines both head and feet (i.e., bows and kneels)*

[3] *That person achieves absolutely nothing who thoughtlessly abandons you*

	Thow stant ordant as sant, of grant maist wyse,	*saint in bestowing favors*
2140	Til be supple and the hie gre of pryce.	*To; support; reward of high price*
	Delyte the tite me quyte of syte to dycht[1]	
	For I apply, schortly, to thy devyse."	*submit, in brief; intention*

The auctor direkit his buke to the rycht
nobill Prynce James the Ferd, Kyng   Fourth
of Scottis.

	Tryumphus laud with palm of victory,	*palm-wreath*
	The laurere crown of infynyte glory,	*laurel*
2145	Maist gracius prince, our soverane James the Ferd,	*Fourth*
	Thy Majesty mot have eternally	*shall*
	Supreme honour, renoun of chevalry,	
	Felycité perdurand in this erd,	*enduring; earth*
	With etern blys in the hevyn by fatal werd.	*decree of destiny*
2150	Resave this rusty, rurall rebaldry,	*smutty, boorish drivel*
	Lakand cunnyng, fra thye puyr lege onlerd,	*Lacking; poor untaught liege*

	Quhilk, in the sycht of thy magnificence,	*Who; sight*
	Confydand in so gret benevolence,	*Trusting*
	Proponis thus my vulgare ignorance,	*Offers*
2155	Maist humely, wyth dew obedyence,	*humbly; due*
	Besekand oft thy mychty excellence	*Beseeching*
	Be grace til pardon all sic variance	*all this sort of error*
	With sum benyng respect of ferme constance,	*kind consideration*
	Remyttand my pretendit negligence	*Forgiving; demonstrable*
2160	Throw quhais mycht may humyll thyng avance.	*whose power; humble; prosper*

	Breif burall quair, of eloquence all quyte,	*Sketchy unrefined book; empty*
	With russet weid and sentence imperfyte,	*coarse apparel; expression*
	Til cum in plane, se thow thow not pretend tha.[2]	
	Thy barrant termis and thy vyle endyte	*sterile words; ugly versifying*
2165	Sall not be min; I wyll not have the wyte.	*mine; blame*
	For, as for me, I quytcleme that I kend tha.	*retract claim to having known you*

---

[1] *Be pleased to rid me quickly of sorrow in order that I may write*

[2] *To come into the open, make sure you do not put yourself forward*

Thow art bot stouth. Thyft lovys lycht but lyte.   *stealth; Theft loves light but little*

Not worth a myte, pray ilk man till amend tha.   *ask each person to; you*

Fare on with syte! and on this wyse I end tha.   *Travel; misery!*

Finis.

Explanatory Notes

1   Concluding his tale of Memnon's death at Troy, Ovid mentions the tears Aurora the dawn-goddess sheds each morning in memory of her son (*Metamorphoses* 13.621–22); the image is conventional in English and Scots courtly verse (Lydgate, *Troy Book* 3.2745–58; Dunbar, *Goldyn Targe* 16).

1–18   Douglas's opening might be translated as follows: "When the pale Aurora with her mournful face wrapped her sable-fringed russet cloak with divine ceremoniousness around the soft bed and worthy tapestry of Flora, kindly queen of flowers in May, I arose to perform my customary ritual, and entered an enclosed garden [which was] illuminated by the sun [so that it was] as lovely as Paradise, and [by] delightful boughs in [their] variety of blossoms, so skilfully had Dame Flora embroidered her heavenly bed (which was sprinkled with many a cluster of rubies, topazes, pearls, and emeralds, soaked in balmy dew and suitably moist), until warm vapors (very fresh and amply supplied, sweet-smelling, of a most fragrant odor) [were] distilling the silver droplets upon the daisies, the greenness of which vapors the branches poured upon the garden paths, chasing away nighttime mists with a smoky incense." The subject phrase "hot vapors" lacks a finite verb phrase, and the antecedent for "which" (*Quhilk*, 17) is unclear. The loose syntax of this opening deserves comparison with the tighter beginning to Chaucer's General Prologue (*Whan . . . Whan . . . Than; Canterbury Tales* 1.1–18), an enticing but inimitable model for ambitious fifteenth-century poets (Pearsall 58–59).

2   The cloak of the dawn-goddess Aurora is both rustic and courtly: made of the coarse reddish-brown wool of peasant clothing, it is nevertheless fringed with costly black fur. This allusion to the colors in the dawn sky may also refer to the mixing of rustic and courtly in the poem as a whole.

6   According to Bartholomaeus Anglicus, "In May woodis wexith grene, medis springith and florischith and wel nyghe alle thingis that beth alyve beth imeved to joye and to love" (*On the Properties of Things* 1.531 [9.13]); Chaucer's Arcite goes into the woods alone at dawn "to doon his obser-

81

vaunce to May," and there he makes "a gerland of the greves, / Were it of wodebynde or hawethorn leves," and sings a song to May (The Knight's Tale, *CT* 1.1499–512).

7   This may simply be a pleasant garden; a *plesance*, however, is a walled garden (like the gardens in *Le Roman de la Rose* or *The Parliament of Fowls*), into which one enters, as Douglas's narrator says he did.

8   Among the marginal emendations written into the National Library of Scotland's black-letter copy (E) is *dilectabil*, at this line; the late-sixteenth- or early-seventeenth-century writer of these emendations perceived a flaw in the repetition of the rhyme-word *amyable*.

11   Along with the pun on *bed* (see also line 4), there is one on *set*, being the name for a cluster of either jewels or buds.

16   In a May scene, Chaucer refers to "silver dropes hangynge on the leves" (The Knight's Tale, *CT* 1.1496).

17–18   The *verdour* being poured out is assumed to be related to the *vapours hote* mentioned before (14); like incense driving away impure thoughts in a church, it drives away the noxious mists of the passing night.

20   Lydgate spoke of a flourishing garden as Nature's tapestry in *The Complaint of the Black Knight* (50–52).

21–24   Birdsong is commonly to be heard in the pleasant place (Curtius 195, 197); following Chaucer (*The Parliament of Fowls* 491–93), English and Scots courtly poets tend to exaggerate the effects of this sound (*Complaint of the Black Knight*, 45–46; *Goldyn Targe* 25; Pearsall 90).

25   L's reading *eccon* is also found in D; however, it is not a spelling found elsewhere and has been regarded as an error stemming from the text from which both L and D are derived. Conceivably the *-n* should be understood as a plural. E reads *Echo*.

30   Ovid names the four horses of the Sun, Eous being the red horse of dawn (*Metamorphoses* 2.153–54); Henryson uses a different source for his description of the four horses (*Testament of Cresseid* 211–16).

32   An echo of Ovid's description of the chariot of the Sun, during the story of Phaethon ("gold was the axle, gold the shaft, and gold was the entire circle of each wheel"; *Metamorphoses* 2.107–08).

49–52   These three deities are allegories for wind, frost, and rain (or flood; see Dunbar's *Thrissil and the Rois* [May 1502 or 1503], 64–66); Saturn is memorably associated with wintry weather in Henryson's *Testament of Cresseid* (155–68).

53   Beryl is proverbially associated with clarity and brightness (Whiting B263).

63   Hearing an authoritative voice (sometimes taken to be a bird's) is a convention in poems about a visit to the pleasant place (e.g., Lydgate's *Seying of the Nightingale*; Henryson's "Praise of Age"; Dunbar's "The Merle and the Nichtingall," "All erdly joy returnis in pane").

65   Calling May the maternal month is a Chaucerism (*Troilus and Criseyde* 2.50; *Court of Sapience* 1269).

89   The dreamer looks up to see something new three more times (784, 1405–06, 1934).

105   Following Aristotle, Bartholomaeus describes several types of *impressiouns*, actually meteorites, but which were believed to be generated in the atmosphere at various altitudes by the ignition of hot dry air: one of these, *ignis longus*, is called "a dragoun spoutynge fire" (*On the Properties of Things* 1.569–70 [11.2]).

108   "Feeble" is a word the dreamer often uses of himself (100, 103, 108, 770, 970, 1166, 2032; Curtius 83).

113–17   According to Bartholomaeus, the "sensible soul" receives sense impressions, has the source of its vital power in the heart, and is the generator of sleep (*On the Properties of Things* 1.98–100 [3.9–12]); it would seem to be this aspect of soul that is affected by the sudden flash of light; Bartholomaeus also discusses those stimuli that cause the blood to rush to the heart to preserve the heat of the body (fear, infection, injury, air pollution, great cold), "whanne the spirit *vitales* fleth his contray and closith himself in the innere parties of the herte" (106).

127–35   See *The House of Fame* 523–28, where Chaucer celebrates his feeble brain, taking off on Dante, *Inferno* 2.8–9. By the later fifteenth century such disclaimers are commonplace.

136–53   Chaucer describes a dream-desert in *The House of Fame* (482–91); a closer parallel to Douglas's wasteland is Chaucer's description of the noisy, barren forest surrounding the temple of Mars (The Knight's Tale, *CT* 1.1975–80); Douglas may also be drawing on the sudden transformation of the forest from pleasant to hellish place that is part of the tradition of the encounter between the Three Living and the Three Dead (Tristram 165).

142   B records A. J. Aitken's emendation *barrane* for L and E's *bare raif*, the *n* having plausibly been mistaken for *u*, with *raif* an alternate spelling for *raue*.

146   The source for the image of yelling fish is "the medieval list of the Signs of Doomsday attributed to St. Jerome and included in Peter Comestor's *Historia Scholastica*" (Nitecki 18–19).

163–92   The ten-line stanza here is the one Henryson uses for the lament of Orpheus (134–83), and the one used in the mid-fifteenth-century Scots translation of a French complaint on the death of Margaret, daughter of James I of Scotland and wife of the Dauphin (*Liber Pluscardensis* 1.382–88); see also the "ballet of inconstant love" later in the poem (607–36).

166   Marginal note in L: *A discription of the inconstance of fortune.*

174–81   Antithesis is a rhetorical figure commonly used to express the variability of Fortune (and of Venus: see lines 601–03; Utley 33; Pearsall 113); another figure employed here (and frequently elsewhere in the poem) is *anaphora,* the repetition of a word or phrase at the beginning of consecutive clauses.

199–300   Gower's Princess Rosiphilee likewise uses a tree as a hiding place from which to watch a procession of a courtly retinue (of Venus); she also stops someone who has failed to obey the laws of that court (*Confessio Amantis* 4.1292–1434).

202   Marginal note in L: *The quen of sapyence wyth hyr court.*

215   Compare Henryson's *goldin listis [edgings] gilt on everie gair* of Jupiter's gown (*Testament of Cresseid* 179).

231   Marginal note in L: *Craftye Synone and false Architefel*; classical and biblical personages are frequently linked in the poem (e.g., 250–51, 338–40, 1453–57).

232   Ahithophel hanged himself after his counsel was rejected (2 Samuel 17:23); see also *Confessio Amantis* 2.3089–94.

246   Biblical heroines: the Apocryphal Book of Judith 8–16; and, for Jael, Judges 4. Chaucer describes Judith's assassination of Holofernes (The Monk's Tale, *CT* 7.2551–74); drawn from antifeminist passages in the *Fall of Princes*; the Lydgatian "Examples against Women" presents Judith as a treacherous woman (Utley 269–70); elsewhere, she is a type of the Virgin Mary (Woolf 130, 279). See *Heroic Women from the Old Testament in Middle English Verse*, ed. Russell A. Peck (Kalamazoo: Medieval Institute Publications, 1991), pp. 109–53, for a fifteenth-century Middle English version of the Judith story, which praises her firm intelligence and strength of character.

251   Marginal note in L: *Wyse and lerned men.*

253   Porphyry, follower of the Neoplatonist philosopher Plotinus; Parmenides, Presocratic Greek philosopher, founder of the Eleatic school of philosophy.

254   Melissus, follower of Parmenides.

255   Shadrach, companion of Daniel and renowned for learning (Daniel 1:4); Secundus, philosopher associated with the Emperor Hadrian; Solinus, late Roman natural historian.

257   Nectanabus, Egyptian magician and reputed father of Alexander the Great; his story is presented at length in Gower's *Confessio Amantis* 6.1789–2366. Hermes Trismegistus, a shadowy figure in Neoplatonist tradition, is the reputed originator of alchemy; see *Confessio Amantis* 4.2606–07 and 7.1476–92.

258   Galen, influential Greek physician; Averroes, Arabic commentator on Aristotle.

259 Enoch and his grandson Lamech, fathers of Methuselah and Noah respectively (Genesis 5:18–19, 21–24; 5:25–31), the former of whom acquired a reputation as an astrologer during the Middle Ages; Diogenes, the Cynic philosopher (see *Confessio Amantis* 3.1201–1311).

261 Flavius Josephus, Jewish leader and historian of the Jewish revolt against Rome (AD 66–70).

262 Melchizedek, priest-king and ally of Abraham (Genesis 14:18–20).

276 Marginal note in L: *Architefel confessis hys owne craftenes deceyt and abused wit.* Ahithophel conspired with Absolom, "And the counsel of Ahithophel . . . was as if a man had enquired at the oracle of God" (2 Samuel 16:20–23); Gower refers to Ahithophel as an example of envy (*Confessio Amantis* 2.3089–94).

283 Virgil has Aeneas recount the strategems by which Sinon deceived the Trojans (*Aeneid* II.57–198).

299 Referring to himself as *elrych* ("elvish"), the poet recalls the Host's jesting description of the pilgrim Chaucer as "elvyssh by his contenaunce" (*CT* VII.703).

308 Marginal note in L: *Feare.*

316–27 Diana's transformation of Actaeon into a hart (*Metamorphoses* 3.131–257; compare the depiction of this event in Chaucer's Temple of Diana, The Knight's Tale, *CT* I.2065–68); and Gower's *Confessio Amantis* 1.333–82.

327 This line is an example of Douglas's concise style: note the asyndeton (omission of a grammatically integral word, here a conjunction between *lord* and *mysknew*), and the grim pun on *batit* (Acteon used to feed his dogs as their master; now he feeds them as their prey); for another example of this style, see line 1680.

329 This is the company to which Cresseid bequeaths her soul in Henryson's *Testament of Cresseid* (587–88).

330   The elephant is an emblem of chastity: "Elephantes hateth the werk of leccherye but oonliche to gendre offsprynge" (*On the Properties of Things* 2.1196 [18.45]).

338   Judges 11.29–40: the Israelite soldier Jephthah vowed to sacrifice to God "whatsoever cometh forth of the doors of my house to meet me" on his victorious return from battle; his daughter was first to meet him, and he "did with her according to his vow" (see also *Confessio Amantis* 4.1505–95 and the Middle English version of the Jephthah story in *Heroic Women from the Old Testament,* ed. Peck).

340   Polixene, daughter of Priam of Troy, sacrificed at Achilles' tomb (*Metamorphoses* 13.447–82). Medieval tradition has Achilles futilely in love with her (*Confessio Amantis* 4.1693–1701; 5.7591–96; 8.2590–96.)

341   Penthesileia, queen of the Amazons, who, for love of Hector, fought at Troy, was killed in battle by Pyrrhus (*Troy Book* 4.3760–4436 and *Confessio Amantis* 4.2135–47; 5.2547–51; 8.2525–27).

342   Iphigenia was offered in sacrifice by her father Agamemnon to Diana (*Metamorphoses* 12.26–39); Virginius killed his daughter to prevent her being raped (Livy, *History* 3.44–48; *Roman de la Rose* 5589–5658; Chaucer, The Physician's Tale; *Confessio Amantis* 7.5131–5306).

346–54 According to Bartholomaeus, "deserte is untiliede and ful of thornes and pricchinge busshes, place of crepyng wormes and venymouse bestes and of wylde bestes, and it is the home of flemyd men and of theves, londe of firste and of drynesse, londe of brennynge and disease, londe of wastynge and of grysnesse, londe of mysgoynge and of errynge" (*On the Properties of Things* 2.721 [14.51]).

359   This is the planet Venus, which appears in the northeast sky before sunrise during late spring and early summer; Taurus (April 20 to May 20) is an astrological house of Venus: "Venus is lord therof by day and the mone by nyght, and Mars partiner with hem" (*On the Properties of Things* 1.466 [8.10]).

360–61 B suggests that the order of these lines as given in L and E be reversed, in order that the relative clause referring to hearing depend on a main clause referring to a sound; this reversal would not affect rhyme scheme. Her suggested emendation has been adopted here.

362   *nowmer.* Number refers to ratios and proportions as well as measure; thus both rhythm and harmony.

364–81   Compare the discourse of Chaucer's Eagle on the properties of sound (*The House of Fame* 765–852).

365–66   Earth is "most passible of elementz . . . . [B]ecause of medlyng of firy and aery parties the erthe is in som parties thynne, holy, and dym and spongy" (*On the Properties of Things* 2.692–93 [14.2]).

373   According to Chaucer's Eagle, "Soun is noght but eyr ybroken" (*The House of Fame* 765).

394   Marginal note in L: *A sorwful harte can not be mery.*

403   Marginal note in L: *Hevinlye harmonye.*

418–35   This set-piece of ekphrasis demonstrates the poet's familiarity with classical models of description, and especially with Ovid's ornate description of the Palace of the Sun (*Metamorphoses* 2.106–10); Douglas imitates lines from this description elsewhere (32, 1837–63; Norton-Smith 243–46). Marginal note in L designates: *Goodly apparell.*

436   L: *thair;* E: *thir. Thair* is probably a variant of the demonstrative *thir* ("these"), rather than the possessive pronoun ("their").

444   In ascending order, the angelic hierarchies are (1) Angels, Archangels, and Virtues; (2) Powers, Principalities, and Dominations; and (3) Thrones, Cherubim, and Seraphim (*On the Properties of Things* 1.68–84 [2.7–18]); the comparison with angels' song is proverbial (Whiting A128).

476–80   Compare Chaucer's more idealized description of the God of Love, who, "al be that men seyn that blynd ys he, / Algate me thoghte that he myghte se" (*The Legend of Good Women* F prologue 237–38); by emphasizing Cupid's blindness, Douglas depicts him as the "personification of illicit sensuality" (Panofsky 121).

491   Marginal note in L: *Musyke.*

492–501   Douglas's *tour de force* of musical technology bespeaks the sophistication of musical training and appreciation in Scottish court society in the early sixteenth century. A generation earlier, Henryson also refers to the music of the spheres by means of a similarly abstruse list of specialized musical terms, including *tonys proportionate, duplar, triplar, diatesseron,* and *dyapason* (*Orpheus*, 226–34; compare *Court of Sapience* 2070–74).

502–05   According to Gower, the retinue of Venus is announced by "a soun / Of bombard and of clarion / With cornemuse and Schallemale" (*Confessio Amantis* 8.2481–83; compare *Court of Sapience* 2091–95). But John Lydgate, in *Reson and Sensualyte* 5564–5612, offers the first extended catalogue of instruments that accompany the entourage of Cupid, Dame Beauty, and their court — *harpys, fythels, rotys, lutys, rubibis, geterns, organys, cytolys, monocordys* (5583), *trumpes, trumpetes, shallys, doucetes, floutys,* etc., with all their "proporsiouns" and "verray hevenly son . . . so hevenly and celestiall" (5601, 5606). See also *The Buke of the Howlat*, where Holland provides a long list of musical instruments, including *psaltery, sytholis, croude* (a kind of fiddle, with two to six strings, a bow and, later, a finger board, played at the shoulder, or, depending on the size, across the knees), *monycordis* (a forerunner of the clavichord, with strings and bridges, at first bowed, but later keyed), *tympane, lute, organis, claryonis* (a kind of trumpet, at first straight, later folded), and *portativis* (a portable organ) (757–67). See also *The Squire of Low Degree* (1069–79), for another catalogue of instruments.

507   B's note on this puzzling line is useful: "*Fractionis* perhaps refers to what Wyclif calls 'a smale brekynge' (*English Works*, ed. F. D. Matthew, *EETS*, 1880, page 191), *i.e.,* a form of singing in which a single long note in plain chant was represented by two or more notes in the accompanying parts; *rest* may have its musical sense of 'an interval of silence'; *clois compell* may perhaps be literally 'drive close together.' A tentative translation is: '[I heard] short notes divided by intervals of silence or sung rapidly in close succession'" (p. 181).

509–10   1 Samuel 16:14–23.

511–12   Ovid refers to Jupiter's mortal son Amphion raising the walls of Thebes by playing his lyre (*Metamorphoses* 6.180). See Chaucer's Manciple's Tale IX.116–18.

513   Possibly alluding to Orpheus.

517–18   A comically overstated admission of ignorance, recalling Henryson's confessions of lack of musical expertise (*Orpheus* 240–42).

518   The cuckoo is a proverbially unmusical bird (Whiting A174).

523   The "music of the spheres" consists of the sounds supposed to be generated by the harmonious revolutions of the planets and stars; according to Bartolomaeus, the outermost sphere in motion (the *primum mobile*; see line 1840 note) "is cause affectif of generacioun and of lyvynge; and ravyschith and drawith to hitsilf contrarye thinges, for by violence of his mevinge he drawith aftir him the planetis, that metith therwith. And passith forth with armonye and acorde; for, as Aristotel seith, . . . of ordinate meovynge of the spere and of contarye metinge of planetes in the worlde cometh armonye and acorde" (*On the Properties of Things* 1.458 [8.6]; see Henryson, *Orpheus*, 220–22).

525   The Welsh bard known as Glasgerion; compare *The House of Fame* 1208, and Child Ballad 67.

534   *of*. L reads *or brounvert;* E: *ovirbrouderit*. E makes easier sense ("embroidered"); it is possible that L's reading *or brounvert* is the preferable one, however, the line then reading "Whose poorest clothing was (made of) silks or dark-green [cloth]." Combinations of *brown* with other terms of color simply indicated that the color thus modified was especially dark (*OED brown*, a.1); and often terms of color could be used by themselves as names of types of cloth (*DOST broun*, n.2; a.1).

550   Marginal note in L: *Mars*.

559–61   On the adulterous love of Mars for Venus, see *Metamorphoses* 4.171–89. See also Chaucer's *Complaint of Mars*.

562–91   Similar catalogues of famous lovers appear in *The House of Fame* 388–426, *The Legend of Good Women* F prologue 249–68, *CT* 2.57–76, and *Confessio Amantis* 8.2500–2656.

562–63   Marginal note in L: *Lovers.* The two noble kinsmen Palamon and Arcite, rivals in love for Emily, sister-in-law of Theseus, Duke of Athens; characters in Chaucer's Knight's Tale.

564   This emphasis on Aeneas' falseness is Chaucerian (*The Legend of Good Women* 1236, 1265–76, 1285–86, 1325–31; *The House of Fame* 255–92; following *Aeneid* 2 and Ovid's *Heroides* 7); compare Douglas's later skepticism on this account: Chaucer "set on Virgill and Eneas this wyte, / For he was evir (God wait) all womanis frend" (*Eneados* 1.prologue 448–49). See also *Confessio Amantis* 4.77–137, where faithless Aeneas is accused of *slowthe.*

565   See Chaucer's *Troilus and Crisyede*, of course, but also Gower's *Confessio Amantis* 2.2456–58; 4.2795–97; 5.7597–7602; and 8.2531–35.

566   While Douglas could have had access through various sources to the story of Helen's abduction to Troy by Paris, this reference appears in a passage relying heavily on Ovid's "Heroines" (*Heroides*), the sixteenth of which is a letter from Paris to Helen, and the seventeenth, Helen's reply.

567   Lucrece, raped by Lucius Tarquinius, commits suicide (*The Legend of Good Women* 1680–1885; *Confessio Amantis* 7.4754–5130; 8.2632–39; Ovid, *Fasti* 2.685–852); the letter of Penelope to her long-lost husband Ulysses is the first of Ovid's *Heroides*; see *Confessio Amantis* 4.147–233 and 8.2621–31.

568   The tale of these ill-starred lovers is told by Ovid (*Metamorphoses* 4.55–166), followed by Gower (*Confessio Amantis* 3.1374–1494) and Chaucer (*The Legend of Good Women* 706–923).

569   Procne's husband raped and mutilated her sister Philomela (*Metamorphoses* 6.426–674; *Confessio Amantis* 5.5551–6074; *The Legend of Good Women* 2228–393).

570   King David loved Bathsheba, wife of his soldier Uriah, and successfully conspired to have Uriah killed in battle in order to marry her (2 Samuel 11:2–27). See *Confessio Amantis* 8.2689–90.

571   Alcione's drowned husband Ceyx appeared to her in a dream (*Metamorphoses* 11.410–748; Chaucer, *The Book of the Duchess* 62–217); and *Confessio Amantis* 4.2927–3123; 8.2647–56.

572–73   While it is possible that Douglas had read a Latin translation of Book I of Homer's *Iliad*, he would have had easier access to the story of Achilles' anger over Agamemnon's appropriation of Briseis through Ovid's many allusions to it (*Heroides* 3; *Amores* 1.9.33, 2.8.11–14; *Ars Amatoriae* 2.399–406; *Remedia Amoris* 467–84, 777–84).

574   Phyllis, a princess of Thrace, fell in love with the Athenian prince Demophon (on his way back from Troy) and married him; feigning a desire to visit his mother, he deserted her, and she cursed him, having given him a love-token to open if away longer than a year; he did so, went mad, and died on his own sword. For Phyllis' letter, see Ovid, *Heroides* 2 (also *Remedia Amoris* 591–604) and *The Legend of Good Women* 2394–2561; for another version of the story (in which Phyllis, having committed suicide, is transformed into a filbert tree), see *Confessio Amantis* 4.731–878).

575   Medea, a sorceress and princess of Colchis, fell in love with Jason and helped him steal the Golden Fleece; returning with Jason to Greece, she restored his father's youth and murdered his enemy Pelias, but then went into exile (*Metamorphoses* 7.1–403; *Confessio Amantis* 5.3368–4222; and *The Legend of Good Women* 1580–1679).

576   An English translation of this French prose romance, *Paris and Vienne,* was printed by William Caxton in 1485.

577   Having been shown how to get through the Labyrinth by Ariadne, Theseus abducted her from Crete and then abandoned her on the island of Naxos (*Metamorphoses* 8.168–82; *Heroides* 10, *The Legend of Good Women* 1886–2227, *Confessio Amantis* 5.5231–5495); Theseus later married another Cretan princess, Phaedra, who fell in love with his son by the Amazon queen Antiope (*Heroides* 4); Gower includes Theseus among the retinue of Venus: "thogh he were untrewe / To love, as alle wommen knewe, / Yit was

he there natheles / With Phedra, whom to love he ches" (*Confessio Amantis* 8.2511–14).

578   There are three English versions of the thirteenth-century romance *Ipomadon* (by Hue de Rotelande), in which the ill-dressed hero pretends to prefer hunting to jousting, only to win in disguise at the tournament, gaining the hand of a princess when he is recognized.

579   Ahasuerus loved Esther (Esther 2:17). Susannah was falsely accused of adultery (Daniel, apocryphal chapter 13; see also *The Pistel of Swete Susan* in *Heroic Women from the Old Testament,* ed. Peck).

580   Delilah, wife and betrayer of Samson (Judges 16.4–20; The Monk's Tale, *CT* 7.2063–70; *Confessio Amantis* 8.2701–04).

581   Deianira, neglected wife and unintentional murderer of Hercules (*Metamorphoses* 9.1–158; *Heroides* 9; The Monk's Tale, *CT* 7.2119–26; *Confessio Amantis* 2.2145–2307; 8.2559–62).

582   Biblis, cursed lover of her twin brother (*Metamorphoses* 9.454–668); Absalom, handsome, rebellious son of David, who likewise was incestuous (2 Samuel 13:1–18.33; *Confessio Amantis* 8.216–22.)

583   After spending two years with her, Hypsipyle's lover Jason departed in search of the Golden Fleece and then fell in love with Medea (*Heroides* 6, *The Legend of Good Women* 1368–1679; Lydgate, *Siege of Thebes* 3188–92); Scylla, lover of her father's enemy, Minos (*Metamorphoses* 8.1–150).

584   Tristram, knight at courts of Kings Arthur and Mark, and lover of Mark's wife Iseult (*Confessio Amantis* 6.471–76, 8.2500–01); Elkanah and Hannah, parents of the prophet Samuel (1 Samuel 1–2).

585   Chaucer's legend of Cleopatra (*The Legend of Good Women* 580–705), in which the Egyptian queen jumps into a snake-pit declaring her love for Mark Antony, would have been available to Douglas (Lydgate follows Chaucer in his version: *Fall of Princes* 6.3620–68). See also *Confessio Amantis* 8.2571–77.

586 Hercules abducted Iole, thereby arousing the jealousy of Deianira (see line 581 note); having died to save her husband, Alcestis was rescued from Hades by Hercules (*Confessio Amantis* 7.1917–43, 8.2640–46), and she is Chaucer's advocate in the Court of Love (*The Legend of Good Women*, G prologue 179, 317–431; F prologue 341–441, 510–16); *Ixion* probably refers to Hesione (rescued by Hercules from a sea-monster; *Metamorphoses* 11.211–17), her name being spelled *Exiona* in line 1598.

587 Griselde, the heroine of Chaucer's Clerk's Tale.

588 Compare *Metamorphoses* 3.339–510, where Narcissus simply pines away; in *Confessio Amantis* 1.2340–42, he dashes his head against a stone after beholding a lovely lady in the water, for whom he yearns.

589–91 Genesis 29.

592–94 The refinement of costume and decay of morals among women is a common antifeminist topic (Utley 60; Pearsall 118–19, 134–35; compare Henryson's more positive approach in "The Garmont of Gud Ladies," and Dunbar's more subtly ironic "Thir ladyis fair that in the Court ar kend," 40–48); see also the self-directed antifeminism of Venus, in lines 981–87.

607 Marginal note in L: *A ballet of inconstant love.*

613 The word *involupit* is peculiar to Douglas (e.g., *Eneados* IV.ii.44 and VII.ii.67, the only two citations of the word in *DOST*); Copland provides an easier reading, *involvit*, which I emend in favor of the more authentic term.

625 In Richard Holland's *Buke of the Howlat*, the complaining owl likewise calls himself a *bysyn*, a bad example, a portent (107, 959); Venus later calls the dreamer "that bysnyng schrew" (943).

627–36 The "Wo worth" anaphora was a commonplace of courtly complaint, originating with *Troilus and Criseyde* 2.344–47. Perhaps the best translation is "Alas." "Woe to" or "Woe befall" or "Woe become" hint at the untranslatability of the idiom.

630 Marginal note in L: *He curseth the worlds felycite, fortune and al his pleasure.*

634–36	Henryson's Cresseid likewise curses "fals Cupide" and his mother Venus (*Testament of Cresseid* 134–35).
641	A *poid* is a toad; the word derives from *poddock (DOST pode, poid)*.
649–52	The dreamer is "mobbed" (Parkinson 502–04); this blackening he undergoes bears comparison with the "spottis blak" with which Cresseid is punished (*Testament of Cresseid* 339).
653–54	These two perform the same function as do two fools in *The Buke of the Howlat*, the Lapwing and the Cuckoo; the names here are also suggestive of birds, *skryme* being a verb used for attacking birds in the *Howlat* ("skrym at myn e"; 67) and in Dunbar's "Fenyeit Freir" (123), and (less plausibly) *chyppynuty* referring to someone who (or something which) breaks nuts. B's suggestion that these names are "nicknames for malicious goblins" (185–86) is supported by one of them being surnamed *fery* ("fairy"). There may be some connection here with the attendants of the Scottish Lords of Misrule (the "King of the Bean" at Epiphany and the "Abbot of Unreason" at Shrovetide and in May), which were called *dablets* (Anna Jean Mill, *Medieval Plays in Scotland* [Edinburgh: William Blackwood, 1927], pp. 313–27).
664–702	Marginal notes in L: *The Auctor accused* (665); *Answer* (684); *Appellationem* (692). This defense conforms to practices of Scottish law (indictment, plea for mercy, declaration of innocence, objection to the competency of the court; see *Habakkuk Bisset's Rolment of Courtis*, ed. Sir Philip J. Hamilton-Grierson [Edinburgh: William Blackwood and Sons, 1920], I, 174). In Henryson's *Fables*, the accused sheep uses similar arguments in his defense (1187–1201).
665	B finds it "unlikely that any specific historical Varius is here alluded to. . . . [The] name seems a punning reference to the traditional fickleness and uncertainty of the love-goddess" (186).
666	The preposition *tyl* ("to") is the common form of the word in early sixteenth-century Scots and appears frequently in L, though not in E; *accusyng* uses the *-ing* suffix to mark the infinitive, an anglicism in Older Scots courtly style (see also 729).
674	The simile is proverbial (Whiting K16).

688–95   In Henryson's "The Sheep and the Dog," the accused sheep likewise objects against his "juge suspect" (*Fables* 1180).

691   A pathetic facial expression is appropriate during an oration (Cicero, *De Oratore* 2.189–96); Lydgate considers it the proper "look" for a poet about to recite (*Siege of Thebes* prologue 175; *Troy Book* 2.870–99).

695   B cites Sir Gilbert of the Haye: "the law sais that it sittis nocht till a womman to mell hir with the thingis that pertenis to jugement of men . . . a thing that is of lawar condicioun may nocht be juge till ane thing that is of hyar condicioun" (*Buke of the Law of Armys* [4.108] 251).

696–99   Douglas attempted this plea (to be tried by a judge who had ecclesiastical jurisdiction) with equal lack of success in 1515, when he was tried for attempting to buy the office of Bishop of Dunkeld (Small 1.lxii–lxiii).

697   This gesture of modesty is conventional (*capitatio benevolentiae*).

706   Marginal note in L: *A thretnyng.*

712   This reference to the poet's first arrival at the Court of Venus may seem an autobiographical allusion; probably it refers, however, to the poet's entry into the pleasant place, at the start of the poem.

716–17   There is a cluster of proverbs ironically referring to the speed and "sharpness" of snails (Whiting S416–17, 421, 425).

718–22   Compare *The Legend of Good Women* F 322–24, where Cupid makes a similar charge against the poet.

731   This is the second reference to facial color (see 652): the dreamer, having had his face daubed with some black substance, turns pale with fear and anxiety.

735   C. S. Lewis saw this as a psychologically revealing detail (*Allegory* 291).

738–44   The fear of transformation is "subtly Ovidian" (B 59).

747–51	Jupiter transformed his paramour Io into a heifer when his wife Juno came along; she kept the heifer under the guard of hundred-eyed Argus until Mercury rescued it (*Metamorphoses* 1.583–746).
749	*yymmyt.* L: *ʒymmyt*, from OE *ʒeman*, to guard, care for, attend, govern.
752–53	The story of Lot's wife, transformed into a pillar of salt for looking back over her shoulder at the destruction of Sodom and Gomorrah (Genesis 19:26), has been mingled with that of the Theban queen Niobe, who continues to weep for her dead children even after she has been turned into marble (*Metamorphoses* 6.146–312).
754–55	In punishment for serving Jupiter human flesh, Lycaon was turned into a wolf (*Metamorphoses* 1.163–64, 209–52).
756	In the height of his pride, King Nebuchadnezzar suddenly became like an animal, "and he was driven from men, and did eat grass as oxen, and his body was wet with the dew of heaven, till his hairs were grown like eagles' feathers and his nails like birds' claws" (Daniel 5:30–33; *Confessio Amantis* 1.2785–3042).
761–62	A topic around which several proverbs have gathered (Whiting M170, S428, W719).
771	An alliterative tag (*DOST bare* 4b; *blis* 1).
772	Marginal note in L: *Consolation.*
775–79	A periphrasis for God, who has prepared a means for the dreamer's rescue because a blessed soul has interceded on the dreamer's behalf.
792	Marginal note in L: *Poetis.*
801	Meters of classical verse, the sapphic being a lyric meter (a favorite of Horace's in his *Odes*), and the elegiac a popular and versatile meter (e.g., for epigrams and inscriptions) which was frequently used by Ovid (as in the *Art of Love* and the Heroides).

802–03   Douglas appears to be referring to a single-stringed monochord of the sort used by Pythagoras to demonstrate the proportions between musical intervals (*Court of Sapience* 2040–58; Marcuse 197); B takes Douglas to mean that the string never slipped out of tune. By the sixteenth century, monochords had several strings and were sometimes keyed. See line 504 and note.

804   The *psaltree* is the lyre; the word is used to translate the Latin *citharis* in line 863.

805–07   "Division of accents" may mean rapid melodic figuration based on a relatively simple sequence of notes; "long measure" would thus be the rhythm of the basic sequence, which is "held," not distorted.

806   *the mesure.* E's reading, which I prefer for metrical reasons. Conceivably L's omission of *the* could indicate that *mesure* was pronounced in three syllables; but early sixteenth century is late for a phonemic *-e.*

808–09   Douglas imagines Ovid's *Heroides* as choral performances. Classical poets were thought of in the fifteenth century as having sung their works to mimed accompaniment (*Troy Book* 2.867–904).

810–15   *Heroides* 2, 1, and 20–21: Acontius tricked Cydippe into swearing to Diana that she would marry no one but him.

819–21   Subtle use of the "colors" (devices) of rhetoric, and maintenance of clear, unvarying meter are singled out here as the prime skills of the poet.

833   *mate* seems an over-familiar way to refer to Venus; the reading in E, *or meit* ("or meet"), does not make sense in context, however.

836   Henryson also lays stress on *polite termes* (Fables 3, 2716; *Testament of Cresseid* 241) in discussing rhetoric.

838–39   At the beginning of his translation of the *Aeneid,* Douglas calls Virgil "flude of eloquens, . . . sweit sours and spryngand well" (1.prologue 4, 9).

840   *Helicon.* L: *hylicon;* E: *Helicon.*

844–46 These paradoxical phrases (pleasure and merriment are fleeting, not stead-fast or constant; joy and discipline might be considered opposites) express "the traditional view of the poet's office: to teach and to delight" (B 57).

852 *Metamorphoses* 5.310 may be the source for naming Thespis as mother of the Muses, whose parentage is usually assigned to Jupiter and Mnemosyne.

854–79 Marginal note in L: *The nyne muses.* B notes that these lines on the functions of the Muses are based closely upon a short Latin poem often included in early editions of Virgil, *De Musarum inventis.*

858–59 In *De Musarum inventis* (and generally in classical tradition), Thalia is the Muse of comedy and eclogue: *wanton wryt* comes from the phrase *lascivo . . . sermone* in the Latin source.

862–65 Terpsichore is more correctly the Muse of dance. Erato is the Muse more commonly associated with the lyre itself, and also with lyric poetry. Douglas owes the confusion to his Latin original.

866–67 More explicitly than does his source, Douglas associates Polyhymnia with command of the colors of rhetoric.

877–78 Perhaps "epic" is a misleading way to translate *heroicus,* which in this context refers to the high courtly style (Blyth, pp. 60–62, 164–67).

881 Nymphs are female personifications of natural objects, those associated with water being called Naiads (among them, the sisters of Narcissus; *Metamorphoses* 3.505–06).

882 E offers a less bizarre reading here: *fair Ladyis for Phanee.* Still, L's reading is explainable in the light of Dunbar's spelling *Phanus* for "Faunus" (*Goldyn Targe* 119); if *Phanee* refers to "fauns," the word cannot be synonymous with the following phrase, "ladyis of thir templis ald," but must rather be the first item in a list of various personages in the retinue of the Muses.

883 The *Pyerides,* the nine daughters of Pierus, rivals to the Muses; Calliope defeated them in a contest of song, and Urania turned them into magpies (*Metamorphoses* 5.293–678); dryads are tree-nymphs (followers of the goddess Ceres; *Metamorphoses* 8.746–50); satyrs are boisterous inhabitants

of forests, often depicted (like their traditionally gentler counterparts in Roman tradition, the fauns) with goat's legs (Marsyas was a satyr who challenged Apollo to a contest in music, and, losing, was flayed by the god; *Metamorphoses* 6.382–400).

884   The Nereids are the sea-maidens, the fifty daughters of the sea-god Nereus and the nymph Doris (*Metamorphoses* 13.742–43); Aonia is a name for Boeotia, where Mount Helicon (home of the Muses) stands — Aonians are thus the Muses' neighbors or attendants; the Napaeae are forest nymphs.

888, 890   Note the close occurrence of the alternative forms *afore* and *tofore* in L; in E, *befoir* is used in both spots.

896–97   Marginal note in L: *Homer*. Like the praises of Homer in *Troilus and Criseyde* (1792) and *The House of Fame* (1466), this probably does not indicate familiarity with *Iliad* or *Odyssey* (Bawcutt, "Library" 111).

898   Marginal note in L: *Virgil and other latin poetis.*

900   Dictys Cretensis and Dares Phrygius, supposed participants in and chroniclers of the Trojan War, the first from the Greek side, the second, from the Trojan.

901   Poggio Bracciolini (1380–1459), Italian humanist, famed for his discoveries of classical manuscripts and notorious for his invectives; it may not be alliteration alone that finds him a place beside the Roman comic poet Plautus and satirist Persius.

902   Although Terence was a Roman author of comedies, his plays were used as school texts for learning Latin grammar; he thus earns a spot with the grammarians Donatus and Servius.

903   The Roman Valerius Flaccus and the Italian laureate Francis Petrarch were both authors of uncompleted epics (*Argonautica* and *Africa* respectively).

904   Aesop and Cato, supposed authors, respectively, of *Fables* and *Distichs,* elementary school-texts in the fifteenth century; Alain de Lille (c. 1127–1203), author of the allegorical poems *Anticlaudianus* and *De planctu naturae.*

905   Douglas may be referring here to Gualterus Anglicus, author of a late twelfth-century Latin version of Aesop which was a principal source for Henryson's *Fables;* Anicius Manlius Boethius is the late Roman philosopher, author of *The Consolation of Philosophy,* widely circulated and translated throughout the Middle Ages.

906   Quintilian (AD 35 – c. 95), whose eminence as a rhetorical authority rose in 1416, when Poggio Bracciolini discovered a complete manuscript of his *Institutio oratoria;* that work was first printed in 1470.

907   Juvenal, the second-century Roman satirist; Chaucer had referred to him as a moral authority (*Troilus and Criseyde* 4.197, *CT* III.1192–94).

908   *mixt* refers to the first-century Roman poet Martial's versatility of mood and meter, as revealed in his *Epigrams*. In a letter mourning the poet's death, the Younger Pliny called him "talented, subtle, penetrating, witty, and sincere."

909   Statius wrote the *Thebaid* (AD 90), an epic on the quarrel between the sons of Oedipus; *bruyt* here may simply be "fame" *(OED* s.v. bruit); but, more specifically, the word means "history," alluding to the medieval English chronicle Brut *(OED* brute, sb²).

910   *Laurence of the vale,* as in E; L reads *Laurence of Vale.* Neither is metrically satisfactory, though L is perhaps preferable. Fausto Andrelini (1462–1518), laureated by the Roman Academy, a humanist poet and editor of Ovid.; Lorenzo Valla (1407–57), humanist philosopher and rhetorician, editor of the Greek New Testament, and adversary of Poggio Bracciolini (see lines 1232–33).

911–12   Giulio Pomponio Leto (1425–98), pupil of Lorenzo Valla and commentator on Virgil; B notes that *fame of late* may refer to this humanist's recent and spectacular funeral.

913   Horace, Roman poet (65–8 BC), whose works (notably the *Odes* and *Satires*) were regaining eminence in the late fifteenth century.

915   *Brunell* may, as B suggests, be the Italian humanist Leonardo Bruni (1369–44); Claudian (late fourth century), the last great Latin poet in the classical

tradition, whose description of the mountain-top home of Venus in *De nuptiis Honorii et Mariae* may have influenced Douglas's description of the palace in Part Three; Giovanni Boccaccio (1313–75), Italian humanist author, best known in late fifteenth-century Scotland and England for his encyclopedic Latin prose works, notably *On the Falls of Illustrious Men (De casibus virorum illustrium),* John Lydgate's version (*The Fall of Princes*) of a French translation of which was commonly referred to as "Bochas."

918 *Brutus Albion* refers to the whole island of Britain, which Douglas elsewhere calls the *yle of Albion (Eneados* XIII. prol. 105, *Conclusio* 11). Brutus was the descendant of Aeneas reputed to have conquered Britain.

919 Marginal note in L: *Chauser and other englyshe and Scottishe Poetis.* For Douglas, Chaucer takes prime place in the conventional fifteenth-century triumvirate of famous English poets (with Gower and Lydgate; Dunbar, *Goldyn Targe* 253–70); he is to English poets what Virgil has come to seem overall when Douglas uses the phrase *a per se* to typify the status of the Latin poet (*Eneados* I. prol. 8).

920 Chaucer gave Gower the epithet *moral (Troilus and Criseyde* V. 1856), and it stuck.

921 The fifteenth-century Benedictine monk John Lydgate was the pre-eminent English poet of the generation after Chaucer, best known for his massive versions of Guido Colonna's *Historia destructionis troiae* (*Troy Book*; 1412–20) and of Boccaccio's *De casibus,* (*The Fall of Princes* 1431–38), and for the dream-visions *The Temple of Glass* and *The Complaint of the Black Knight* (known in Scotland as *The Maying or Disport of Chaucer*); in the prologue to his *Siege of Thebes,* Harry Bailly leads the returning Canterbury pilgrims in laughing at the monk Lydgate when they see him riding abstractedly along (70–91).

923 The pairing of the Scottish poets Walter Kennedy and William Dunbar may allude to their collaborative performance *The Flyting of Dunbar and Kennedie,* an exchange of scurrilous verse invectives; this possibility is strengthened by the reference in the next line to *Quyntyne*, a shadowy figure at the Scottish court, named as Kennedy's second in the *Flyting.* Unlike most of the authors in this catalogue, these two are *yit undede,* Dunbar being heard

of until 1513, Kennedy being referred to as "in poynt of dede" in Dunbar's lament *Timor mortis conturbat me* (c. 1505).

924   The word *huttok* is obscure. It may be related to the equally obscure English word *hattock*, which *OED* glosses as "a small hat," *-ock* being the Scots diminutive suffix; *DOST,* on the other hand, goes no further than to query the word. This *huttok* is something distinctive about Quintin, and may possibly be a badge of some office at the Scottish court.

944   Marginal note in L: *Venus complaint.*

960   The declaration of *chakmate* against persons derives from Chaucerian tradition (e.g., *Troilus and Criseyde* 2.752; *Fall of Princes* 1. prol. 26).

961–66   This defense parallels that made by Alceste on behalf of the dreamer Chaucer to the God of Love (*The Legend of Good Women* F prologue 431–41).

969   Calliope is recommending that the dreamer serve as Venus' herald, proclaiming her commands to every region.

973   "Without prayer or price" is proverbial (Whiting P370).

981   Marginal note in L: *Mercy becumys all men and specily gentylwemen.*

983–87   A conventional set of antifeminist comparisons: in Walter Bower's continuation of the Scottish history *Scottichronicon* (c. 1449) appear similar comparisons with dragons and devils (2.376); the balade "Devise, prowes, and eke humilitee" (recurrent in sixteenth-century compilations of Scots verse) calls a wife "Thou devillis member, thou cursit homycide, / Thou tigir tene, fulfild of birnyng fyre, / . . . . Thou cocatras, that with the sicht of thy ire / Affrayit has full mony a gudely syre" (*Chepman and Myllar Prints,* p. 146; Utley 124).

987   These "wise clerks" are the ones who only a little while before Venus had called "sharp as snails" (717).

991   The line may be corrupt, as B suggests; on the other hand, this may be an intricate example of *hyperbaton*, the distortion of expected word-order.

1015–35   The rhetorical figure most heavily relied upon here is *periphrasis*, the multiplication of synonymous words and phrases.

1016   Marginal note in L: *a ballat for venus plesour*.

1041   A *shower* as an onset of grief or suffering is an example of pathetic fallacy, one of the rhetorical colors of the Scots courtly style.

1048   As B points out, L's reading *campion* is more respectful and appropriate to the situation than E's *companioun*.

1058   An example of Douglas's mingling of Christian doctrine and classical-mythological lore: the dreamer will pray to God to bless the Muse Calliope.

1065   Marginal note in L: *Thankesgyvyng*.

1071   Like the dreamer, this Nymph is never named in the poem. Having been entrusted into her care, he calls her "my keeper," and indeed she has to guide and even carry him past danger (1309–11, 1339–41 1926–29). She is also his "governour" (1169), an instructor from whom he learns the significations of objects he sees on his journey; she functions as does the Eagle in *The House of Fame*. This Nymph is no meek, willowy little thing: she can lift the dreamer (by his hair, if necessary; 1340), and does not hesitate to scold and insult him when he does not keep up with her (1308, 1866–68, 1936–38).

1073   The woodbind or common honeysuckle is associated with Maying (The Knight's Tale, *CT* 1.1508).

1081–84   Marginal note in L: *The auctours vyage*. A similar formula for movement through varied landscapes occurs at line 1246. The aerial perspective is somewhat akin to Geoffrey's flight in *The House of Fame*.

1086–89   This list of nations, zigzagging across Europe, recalls a similarly chaotic sequence in the early sixteenth-century Scots burlesque poem *Lichtoun's Dreme* (28–30).

1092–134   Ovid lists rivers in his description of the disastrous flight of Phaethon (*Metamorphoses* 2.213–73); Bartolomaeus provides a substantial catalogue of mountains (*On the Properties of Things* 2.695–717 [14.3–44]); Boccaccio lists both in his geographical dictionary *De montibus, silvis, fontibus, lacubus, fluminibus, stagnis seu paludibus, et de nominibus maris* (1350–60).

1093–94	The Greek city Pisa (in the western Peloponnese); nearby, Alpheus flows underground into the sea (*Metamorphoses* 5.639–41; Boccaccio 96–97).
1095	In the midst of a list of French rivers, *France* itself seems out of place.
1096	*goldin sandyt* is a conventional epithet for the Spanish river Tagus (*Metamorphoses* 2.251).
1097–98	Ovid describes Hercules' funeral pyre on Mount Oeta (*Metamorphoses* 9.229–38; also Boccaccio 38).
1099	Peneus is the largest river of Thessaly in Greece, flowing between the mountains Olympus and Ossa (Boccaccio 150–51).
1100	Tmolus is a mountain in Lydia (a kingdom on the mainland of Turkey), not Cilicia (further to the south), where Douglas (following Boccaccio 51) puts it (*Metamorphoses* 2.217).
1102	Mount Parnassus and the Castalian spring that flows from it were associated with worship of the Muses; the epithet *twa toppyt* is conventional (*Metamorphoses* 2.221).
1103	Haemus and Rhodope were the mountains on which Orpheus sojourned after losing his wife Eurydice for the second time (*Metamorphoses* 10.77; 2.219, 222).
1105	Mount Carmel (on the northern coast of Israel) was associated with the prophets Elijah and Elisha (1 Kings 18:19, 2 Kings 2:25), the former of whom had reputedly established a monastic community there (Boccaccio 17).
1107	The founding of the monastic Order of the Carmelites is dated in the mid-twelfth century.

1108–09   Located on the remote southeastern shore of the Black Sea, the river Thermodon was the home of the Amazons, a nation of warlike women (*Metamorphoses* 9.190; Boccaccio 164).

1110–12   Mimas, a range in Asia Minor (*Metamorphoses* 2.222; Boccaccio 35); Cithaeron, a range on the Greek mainland (*Metamorphoses* 2.223; Boccaccio 21).

1113   As B (195) shows, this description of Mount Olympus closely echoes that given by Boccaccio (38).

1114   Boccaccio describes Melas as a river in Greece, sacred to Minerva (137; see also *Metamorphoses* 2.247).

1116   The Tanais, or Don, River marked the boundary between Europe and Asia (*Metamorphoses* 2.242; Boccaccio 162–63).

1117   Sperchius, a Thessalian river which Ovid calls *Spercheides* (*Metamorphoses* 2.250; compare Boccaccio 161).

1118   Probably the Syrian river Orontes (*Metamorphoses* 2.249; Boccaccio 146); Douglas's version of the name (*Achicorontes*) can perhaps be explained as a misreading of Ovid's *arsit Orontes*.

1119   Ida, near Troy on the northwest shore of Turkey (*Metamorphoses* 2.218; Boccaccio 30).

1120   According to the Vulgate Bible, Noah's Ark landed upon the hills of Armenia (Genesis 8:4); the Euphrates is one of the great rivers of Mesopotamia, and is the fourth river of Eden (Genesis 2:14).

1123   Mount Dindyma, in Phrygia (west-central Turkey), on which stood a shrine to the goddess Cybele (*Metamorphoses* 2.223; Boccaccio 23–24).

1125   Scythia is the ancient name given to the land north and east of the Caspian Sea.

1126	Tigris is one of the great rivers of Mesopotamia, and (called *Hiddekel*) was named the third river flowing out of Eden (Genesis 2:14); Pison runs into the Black Sea, and was named the first river of Eden (Genesis 2:11).
1127	For this pairing, see *Metamorphoses* 2.257.
1128	Modin was a fortified town in mountainous country in Judaea (1 Maccabees 2:23, 13:30, 16:4; 2 Maccabees 13:14).
1129	Helicon, mountain in Greece dedicated to the Muses, on which the Hippocrene fountain springs; calling this spring *facund*, Douglas refers to the wealth of eloquence it imparts to the one who drinks here.
1130	Eryx, a mountain in western Sicily, the site of a temple to Aphrodite (*Metamorphoses* 2.221, 5.363); Acheron, a river of the Underworld, as well as one which emerges from a gorge in western Greece, neither of which are normally associated with Venus.
1133	Birthplace of Apollo, on the island of Delos.
1134	Unless the Muses have doubled back towards Mount Helicon (line 1129), there seems to be a distinction made between Hippocrene and Caballine fountains, two names which are usually taken as synonymous.
1141–43	The dreamer re-enacts a common rhetorical gesture of modesty, derived from Persius, *Satires*, prologue 1.
1150	In English and Scots courtly verse, descriptions of the "pleasant place" typically include details about clear water flowing over a glittering streambed (*Goldyn Targe* 36; *Complaint of the Black Knight* 78). The phrase *sterny greis* (compare E: *stanerie greis*) is hard, *greis* usually referring to steps.
1156–59	B provides a gloss for this obscure sentence: "Whoever imprints within his heart their fresh beauty, fair appearances . . . [i.e., if anyone could do this] it would almost cause a wise man to swoon."
1160	*writhyt*. The women's beauty is so dazzling that even Nature is thrown into confusion. *Wrythyst* 2 ppt. of *wryith*, to writhe, twist, wrench out of position.

1162–66   Having finished his description of the pleasant place, Douglas breaks off his description of the Muses with this rhetorical confession of the inexpressibility of his subject (Pearsall 144).

1173   Marginal note in L: *The gates.*

1181–83   An interlude is a play short and simple enough to stage to present between the courses of a banquet; it may consist largely of debate over an important ethical question, interspersed with moments of knockabout farce; ethical debate and farce are suitable counterparts, as the following performances demonstrate.

1186–87   In *The House of Fame*, Chaucer calls Ovid "Venus clerk" (1487); Douglas gives him the Scottish court office of Clerk of Register, and emphasizes his connection with heroic subjects.

1189   Marginal note in L: *Valiant Knightis.* The laurel crown is the badge of literary pre-eminence (Bawcutt, *RES*).

1192   Ovid provides a brief list of the Labors of Hercules, including his descent and return from Hades: *Metamorphoses* 9.182–99.

1195–96   Chaucer (drawing on Boccaccio and Statius), not Ovid, refers to this war (*CT* I.866–67).

1197   *Metamorphoses* 8.169–71.

1198–1200   *Metamorphoses* 4.610–5.249.

1201–03   *Metamorphoses* 8.270–546.

1204–06   *Metamorphoses* 11.751–95.

1207–15   *Metamorphoses* 12.64–145.

1216–21   Referring to *Metamorphoses, Heroides, Ars Amatoria,* and *Remedia Amoris.*

1225   Marginal note in L: *Poetis.*

1226   In Virgil's *Eclogue* 2, the shepherd Corydon is a would-be lover; he wins
            the verse competition of *Eclogue* 7, to which Daphnis listens; Daphnis is
            sung to in *Eclogue* 8.

1227–28   Refers to Terence's comedy *Eunuchus*.

1229–30   Juvenal's behavior is what is expected of a satirist at court; it is the posture
            William Dunbar assumes in his court satires addressed to James IV ("Off
            benefice, Sir, at everie feist" 7; "Schir, yit remember as befoir" 7–10).

1231   *Coquus* ("the cook") was Martial's medieval nickname. As a satirical
            epigrammatist, he frequently "roasts" the people about whom he writes.

1232–33   Poggio Bracciolini wrote Invectives against Lorenzo Valla, his rival in
            scholarship.

1239   *Canterbury Tales* 1.199, on the sweating Monk, may be the source for this
            simile.

1244   David was anointed king of Judah at Hebron (2 Samuel 2.1), where the
            sepulchres of Adam, Abraham, Isaac, and Jacob were reputedly located, and
            where the "dry tree" stood which will come into leaf when the Christians
            conquer the Holy Land (*Mandeville* 47, 49); Adam was traditionally held to
            have been created "in the feeld of Damyssene" (The Monk's Tale, *CT*
            7.2007).

1245   The valley of Jehoshaphat, where, during the Last Judgment, the heathen
            shall be gathered (Joel 3:2, 12–13).

1249–51   The exact location of this *plesand roch* is unclear; it may be significant that
            the two places last named (Hebron and Damascus; 1244) are in the Holy
            Land rather than the world of Greek antiquity, since arriving at this moun-
            tain calls for a prayer of thanksgiving to God.

1254   The trembling pen is a Lydgatian topic of modesty (*Troy Book* 1.4426–28,
            Fall of Princes 1.5517–18; Pearsall 145); see also line 1283.

1255–58   The trembling poetic narrator takes off on 1 Corinthians 2:9.

1259–62	From *Aeneid* 6.625–27: there, the Sibyl is claiming inability to catalogue to Aeneas the torments of the damned in the fortress of Dis.
1264–66	From 2 Corinthians 12:2–3. Chaucer likewise draws on this passage, *The House of Fame* 980–82.
1267–75	Douglas's English contemporary John Skelton has similar comments on disparagers of his work: "For the gyse nowadays / Of sum jangelyng jays / Is to discommende / That they can not amende" (*Garlande or Chapelet of Laurell* 1261–64; likewise Stephen Hawes, *Pastime of Pleasure* 792–819).
1269	The assertion that dreams are "not worth a mite" is proverbial (Whiting D387, M611).
1288–96	Marginal note in L: *Invocacion.* For a brief history of the formulae of invocation of the Muses, see Curtius 232 n., 234, 239.
1298–99	The hill is a maze of error, and only one path will reach the summit; the image is based on a well-established distinction between heresy and true faith (Doob 76–78).
1300–01	The mountain on which Chaucer's House of Fame stands is like "alum de glas" (1124).
1322–23	If Douglas is following Homer, he does so at some remove from his ultimate source, according to which, Hera (Juno) gets Hephaestus (Vulcan) to use fire against the river Xanthus in Achilles' fight against it (*Iliad* 21.328–82).
1336	Marginal note in L: *Idyll people punyshed.*
1338–40	In the apocryphal conclusion to the Book of Daniel ("Bel and the Dragon"), an angel lifts the prophet Habakkuk by his hair in order to carry him to the imprisoned Daniel (Vulgate Daniel 14:23).
1354	L's reading *palyce* is taken to mean "dwelling place" here (see line 52); the word sets up a contrast between this destination and the far happier one up ahead.

1380–82   Marginal note in L: *Faythles peopill.* On shipwreck as an emblem for the destruction of the faithless, see 1 Timothy 1:19.

1387   From St. Paul's Epistle to the Ephesians 2:3.

1393–94   Douglas is expounding a doctrine of salvation through faith and good works; in the prologue to Book II of his translation of the *Aeneid*, he similarly emphasizes that a sinner must act well in order to merit grace (155–68).

1401   This is Douglas's ideal of eloquence (Bawcutt, *Douglas* 86, 160, 206).

1410   This admission that one's writing does no more than blacken paper is commonplace in Lydgate (Pearsall 145, 149); compare Douglas's earlier modest references to his pen (1254, 1283).

1411   A highly traditional topic of continuation (The Knight's Tale, *CT* 1.886–87; *Troy Book* 5.2927–31; Bawcutt, *Douglas* 169).

1413–27   The pleasant place at its most Edenic (Curtius 192, 200): lion and lamb together (Isaiah 11:6), and all plants in season (Genesis 2:9).

1424   As Norton-Smith points out (252), the correct reading at the end of this line is *fare,* meaning "disturbance" *(MED fare* n.6).

1426   Marginal note in L: *The discription of the palace.*

1429–37   The "enumeration of technical details" is a rhetorical convention in the description of buildings (*The House of Fame* 1189–94; *Court of Sapience* 2.1485–89; Norton-Smith, 242–43); in a paper read at a session of the International Congress on Medieval Studies at Kalamazoo (May 1989), Alasdair MacDonald suggested that Douglas based his description on the new Palace at Stirling Castle, with its great hall, gardens in the ward, pools and ditches, and Collegiate Church (*Exchequer Rolls* lxx, 18, 142, 144, 297, 314–17; *Treasurer's Accounts* cclxvi).

1433   While *torris* may refer to "towers," the context is a list of architectural ornament (see *OED s.v. Tore,* "an ornamental knob").

1437   *spryngis* is a variant of *springer*, a term for the moulding on which one foot of an arch is based (Norton-Smith 252).

1444–47   King James IV of Scots was an ardent enthusiast of tournaments (Fradenburg 153–71).

1452   Chaucer's Palace of Fame is made entirely of "ston of beryle" (*The House of Fame* 1184).

1453–54   Bezaleel and Aholiab, divinely-inspired builders of the Tabernacle, the temple of the Israelites, containing the Holy of Holies, the place of the Ark of the Covenant (Exodus 31:2–6; 36:1–38:23; 25:33–34).

1455   On Solomon's building of the temple at Jerusalem, see 1 Kings 6:1–36.

1456   Probably refers to the building of the walls of Troy by the gods Apollo and Neptune, mentioned by Horace (*Odes* 3.3.21). See the earlier reference to Amphion, lines 511–12.

1457   Possibly drawn from *CT* 3.498–99, where Apelles is named as the maker of the tomb of Darius of Persia.

1473   Because of repetition of the word *twelf*, the line in L is hypermetrical, going against Douglas's practice of maintaining a ten-syllable line.

1475   Marginal note in L: *Venus mirrour.*

1483–85   Various jewels have the power to staunch the flow of blood: cornelian (*corneolus*), hematite (*emachite*), heliotrope (*eliotropia*), jasper, pearl (*margarita*), sapphire, smaragdus, and topaz (*On the Properties of Things* 2.843–77 [16.33–95]).

1492   A legendary mirror which enabled the Romans to see whether neighboring countries intended peace or war (see also *Confessio Amantis* 5.2031–2224; *The Buke of the Sevyne Sagis* 1650–76).

1493–94   In this mirror Canacee could discover oncoming danger and distinguish between friend and foe (The Squire's Tale, *CT* 5.132–36).

1500   *in the erth ysent* refers to Adam's banishment from Paradise (Genesis 3: 23–24).

1503   B points out that *subversyoun* echoes a reference ("de subversione urbium"; Genesis 19:29) in the Latin Vulgate Bible to the fall of Sodom.

1505   The medieval tradition that Moses' face was *horned* (rather than *shining*) when he descended from Sinai derives from the Vulgate text at Exodus 34:29. Douglas anticipates when he mentions Moses' horns and "ald Ebrew law" before alluding to the Plagues and the crossing of the Red Sea.

1506   According to Exodus 7–12, ten plagues took place: E's reading is thus preferable to L's *Twelf;* "thair trespas" refers to the obstinacy of the Egyptians in the Biblical narrative.

1507–10   The story is told in Exodus 14.

1509   Marginal note in L: *A lang catathaloge of nobyll men and wemen both of scriptur & gentyll stories.*

1511   The Israelites under Moses were condemned by God to wander for forty years in the wilderness (Numbers 14:33; Deuteronomy 29:5).

1512   These "wars" (notably against Jericho) are the subject of Joshua 6–12.

1514   See Judges 11 for the Israelite warrior Jephthah (whom Douglas mentioned before, line 338), and Judges 6–8 for Gideon.

1515   In order to become king, Gideon's bastard son Abimelech murdered all his seventy brothers except the youngest, who escaped (Judges 9:1–5).

1517–19   The Israelite hero Samson killed a thousand of his Philistine enemies with the "a new jawbone of an ass" (Judges 15:15); he carried off the gates to the city of Gaza (Judges 16:3); and he pulled down the house (not the temple) of the Philistines, killing himself and three thousand of his enemies (Judges 16:22–30).

1520–21   Shamgar killed six hundred Philistines (Judges 3:31; according to the King James Version of the Bible, his weapon was an ox-goad, not a ploughshare as in the Vulgate).

1522–23   Samuel anointed Saul to signify he would be king (1 Samuel 10:1).

1523–24   1 Samuel 14:6–20.

1525–26   1 Samuel 17:40–51. The weight of Goliath's spearhead is given in 1 Samuel 17:7 (six hundred shekels, two shekels to an ounce).

1527–29   2 Samuel 21:16–22. Four giants (a brother and a nephew of Goliath, as well as his sons Ishbibenob — Vulgate Jesbibenob — and a nameless son with six digits on each hand and foot) are defeated by four followers of the aging King David.

1530   1 Samuel 17:34–37.

1531–32   David's "three mighty men" defeated the Philistines despite being ambushed by them on several occasions; Adino killed eight hundred at once (2 Samuel 23:8–12; compare the Vulgate version of verse 8, in which David himself is said to be one of three who killed eight hundred).

1533–39   For David's champion Benaiah (Vulgate Banaias), see 2 Samuel 20–21: he killed two lions, a lion in a pit, and an Egyptian warrior.

1540   Marginal note in L: *Salomon*.

1542–45   Because Rehoboam refused to be kind to his people, all the tribes except those of Judah and Benjamin rejected his kingship (1 Kings 12:13–19).

1546–48   2 Kings 19:35 (the Vulgate has 185,000 as the number slain); for the "gret bost," see 2 Kings 19:10–13.

1549–50   God grants the dying King Hezekiah fifteen more years of life; Isaiah heals the King (2 Kings 20:6–7).

1550–51   Elijah's ascent to heaven is witnessed by his successor Elisha (2 Kings 2:11).

1552   Ezra 7–10:17; Nehemiah 1–7:5, 13.

1553   Daniel 6.

1554   Referring to the apocryphal chapter "Bel and the Dragon" (Daniel 14 in the Vulgate Bible).

1555   The three young Israelites Shadrach, Meschach, and Abednego, condemned by the Babylonian king Nebuchadnezzar to burn in a fiery furnace for refusing to worship a golden statue (Daniel 3).

1556   The deportation of the Israelites into Babylon (2 Kings 24:14, 25:11), *transmigration* being the specialized term used in the Vulgate for this (Ezra 6:16; 8:35).

1558–62   The story told in the apocryphal Book of Tobit (Vulgate Tobias): Tobias is to become the eighth husband of Sarah, but unless he manages to "unbind Asmodaeus the evil demon from her" (3:17), he will suffer the same fate as the seven previous husbands; the angel Raphael advises him to drive the demon away with the smell of the burning heart and liver of a fish (6:10–18).

1563–64   Having gone into the encampment of the Assyrian general Holofernes and been entertained by him, Judith beheaded him (the apocryphal Book of Judith 7–15).

1565–66   Based on Jonah 1:17 and 2:10; B notes that Douglas may be indebted to Chaucer for the notion that Jonah was "schot furth" at the inland city Nineveh (*CT* 2.486–87).

1568–69   Given the Biblical context of this reference to the Macedonian conqueror Alexander the Great, it is likely (as B suggests) that Douglas is relying on the summary of Alexander's career at the beginning of the apocryphal First Book of Maccabees (1:1–8).

1570–71   The oppression of the Jews by the Greek king Antiochus Epiphanes is summarized in 1 Maccabees 1:21–67.

1572–74   Judas Maccabeus ("The Hammer"), whose exploits are the subject of 1 Maccabees 3–9:18 and 2 Maccabees 8–15.

1575–76   Jonathas is the subject of 1 Maccabees 9:28–13:23; Simon, of 13:1–16:22.

1577–84   Douglas need not have drawn directly on Statius' *Thebaid* for this summary; see lines 2120–2235 of *Siege of Thebes* for Lydgate's account of the Theban ambush of Tydeus, and lines 4028–46 for the fate of Amphiorax (also *Troilus and Criseyde* 2.104–05).

1581–82   Theseus' victory at Thebes is summarized in Chaucer's Knight's Tale (*CT* 1.986–90; see also *Siege of Thebes* 4525–53).

1585–87   *Canterbury Tales* 1.896–964; as B notes, however, Lydgate provides a more exact source for the phrase "all barfute" (*Siege of Thebes* 4469). The marginal note to these lines in L reads *Faythfull & constent women.*

1588–93   The ironic praise of women is a hallmark of Lydgate's style: see *Siege of Thebes* 4448–52, *Fall of Princes* 1.4719–816, and further, Pearsall 118–19, 134–36, 216–18).

1594–96   The Centaur's attempted abduction of Pirithous' bride from the wedding feast and the ensuing brawl are described in gory detail in *Metamorphoses* 12.210–530. See also *Confessio Amantis* 6.485–529.

1597–1602   For Hercules's rescue of Hesione and his revenge on her ungrateful father Laomedon, see *Metamorphoses* 11.211–15 and *Confessio Amantis* 5.7195–7224 and 8.2515–24.

1603–05   Medea, sorceress and princess of Colchis, enabled Jason to steal the Golden Fleece from her country (*Metamorphoses* 7.1–158; *Confessio Amantis* 5.3247–4222; *Troy Book* 1.131–3714).

1606   Hypsipyle, princess of Lemnos, whom Jason bedded and then left behind on his way to the Golden Fleece (*Siege of Thebes* 3188–92).

1607–11   Having referred already (1597–1602) to Ovid's version of the Greek overthrow of the Trojan king Laomedon, Douglas alludes to Lydgate's version (*Troy Book* 1.3718, 4063–4307), or Gower's (*Confessio Amantis* 5.7195–7224).

1612–14   Disputing over the Golden Apple of Discord (to be awarded to the most beautiful), the goddesses Juno, Minerva, and Venus appealed to the judgment of the most handsome of men, Paris, who awarded the apple to Venus and earned the hatred of the two others (*Heroides* 16.51–88; *Confessio Amantis* 5.7400–7588; *Troy Book* 2.2520–2809).

1619–20   The sea-nymph Thetis disguised her son Achilles as a girl so that he would not be called to Troy; Ulysses tricked him into revealing his identity (*Metamorphoses* 13.162–73; *Confessio Amantis* 5.2961–3201).

1628–29   After a digest of events in the Trojan War, Douglas draws upon Virgil's *Aeneid*, Book 2, for these details.

1630–56   An interesting summary of the *Aeneid*, much of which (1637–46) concerns Book 6, on Aeneas' journey to the Underworld. By contrast, Chaucer had given most attention to Book 4 (the story of Dido and Aeneas) in his summary (*The House of Fame* 143–467).

1641   Traditionally, the Underworld contains five rivers, rather than four: Styx, Acheron, Cocytus, and (further down) Phlegethon, as well as Lethe.

1643   Sisyphus was condemned by Jupiter to push a stone to the top of a hill only to have it roll back each time (*Metamorphoses* 4.459, 13.27; *Aeneid* 6.616).

1644   The Elysian Fields, where the blessed souls dwell (*Aeneid* 6.640–59). Douglas echoes this line in *Eneados* 6. prol. 100.

1645–46   Anchises' revelations concerning the future greatness of Rome (*Aeneid* 6.756–885).

1647–51   *Aeneid* 7.5–7. For all his insistence on conciseness, Douglas is hardly briefer than Virgil here.

1652   *Aeneid* 7.107–16. Extreme hunger had been predicted for Aeneas and his people before they reached their destination (3.255).

1653–54   The couplet echoes *The House of Fame* 147–48: "In Itayle, with ful moche pyne, / Unto the strondes of Lavyne."

1656   Turnus, Aeneas' fiercest adversary in the battle for Latium; his death ends the work.

1657   Livy's *History of Rome* 1.4–7.

1658–59   Livy's *History of Rome* 1.60 (244 years).

1660–65   Marginal note in L: *Chast Lucretia.* The rape of Lucretia by Sextus, son of King Lucius Tarquinius ("The Proud"), led to Brutus driving the offending family from Rome and abolishing the monarchy (Livy, *History of Rome* 1.57–60). See also *Confessio Amantis* 7.4593–5130.

1671–74   Marginal note in L: *The constancye of Marcus regulus.* Marcus Regulus, captured by the Carthaginians and sent to Rome to urge peace, advised the Romans to fight on, and returned to Carthage to die in captivity (Horace, *Odes* 3.5). The motif of "common profyt" (1674, 1678) that Douglas emphasizes here reminds one of Genius' emphasis on that theme in his discussion of good rule in *Confessio Amantis*.

1675   Servius Tullius, the sixth king of Rome and a good ruler, murdered by Lucius Tarquinius (Livy, *History of Rome* 1.39–48).

1676–80   Having heard the oracle that a chasm in the Forum would not close until Rome's greatest strength was sacrificed, Marcus Curtius leapt into the chasm (Livy, *History of Rome* 7.6); L's reading *Quincyus* (1676) may derive from confusion between this hero and the Roman historian Quintus Curtius.

1684–86   Scipio Africanus, hero of the Second Punic War, took Spain and defeated the Carthaginian general Hannibal (Livy, *History of Rome* 26.46; 30.32).

1688–89   Jugurtha, usurper of the North African kingdom of Numidia, object of repeated Roman attacks, finally captured and executed; the story is told by the Roman historian Sallust (*The Jugurthine War*).

1690–91   Having been defeated by Cicero in his bid to be elected consul, the disreputable Catiline embarked on rebellion and was defeated and killed; Sallust tells the story (*The War of Catiline*).

1692	This civil war is the subject of Lucan's epic *Pharsalia*; Chaucer refers to him and his poem (*The House of Fame* 1497–1502; *CT* 2.401, 7.2719).
1700–01	In this stanza, attention shifts from history to the present and future, apocalyptically considered. The Devil's growing success at winning souls is vividly depicted in Dunbar's "Renunce thy God and cum to me"; likewise, belief in the imminent appearance of the Antichrist is the context for Dunbar's "Lucina schynnyng in silence of the nicht."
1702	As did the catalogue of poetic recitations in the Second Part (1190–1233), the present list now moves from heroic deeds and serious matters to recreations and pastimes.
1709	There appears to be a distinction here between the adjectival verb ending *-ing* (*questyng*) and the present participle ending *-and* (*syrchand*).
1711	*Rauf Coilyear,* a late fifteenth-century Scots romance in alliterative stanzas, a tale about the encounters between a coal-pedlar and Emperor Charlemagne (incognito), in which emphasis is placed on burlesque of courtly conventions. See Alan Lupack's *Three Middle English Charlemagne Romances* (Kalamazoo: Medieval Institute Publications, 1990), pp. 161–204.
1712	*John the Reeve,* a northern English verse-tale similar in plot and tone to the preceding romance; *Colkelbie's Sow,* a late fifteenth-century Scots sequence of three burlesque tales.
1713	Douglas may be referring to a localized version of one of the widespread folktales in which a wren plays a prominent part: nineteenth-century Scottish versions of "The Battle of the Birds and the Beasts" and "The King of the Birds" have been recorded (Campbell 1.49, 53, 285; Armstrong 135–37, 143–44, 202–03); he may also be referring to a particular manifestation of the custom of the "Hunting of the Wren," in which boys hunted and killed a wren on St. Stephen's Day (26 December), and then carried it in a funeral procession, singing a song (Herd 2.209–11). Ailsa Crag, a rocky islet north of the Isle of Man in the Irish Sea west of Galloway, is particularly noted by early chroniclers and travellers for its abundance of sea birds.
1714	Passus 6 of *Piers Plowman* seems out of place in this list of burlesque and popular tales; its inclusion here as a story in which Piers invites Hunger to

pacify some rebellious laborers suggests that at least parts of Langland's work may have been valued as comedy by Douglas's audience.

1715   Goll Mac Morna, leader of the Fianna Fiall, the bodyguard of the High King of Ireland; and Finn Mac Cumhal, who took the place of Goll (his father's slayer) at the head of the Fianna and became one of the great heroes of Ireland. The Gaelic-speaking districts of West and North Scotland retained familiarity with Irish traditions well into the nineteenth century (Campbell 1.xxii–iv, xlvi, xciii, 4.47, 242). Lowland Scots were at least acquainted with these personages: an early sixteenth-century Edinburgh poem refers to Finn as a giant who "dang the devill and gart him yowle; / The skyis ranyd quhen he wald scowle / And trublit all the aire" ("Maner of the Crying of ane Playe" 33–36; *Asloan Manuscript* 2.150).

1717   B cites poem 68 of the Maitland Quarto manuscript, in which the "triumphant nobill fame" of Sir Richard Maitland is mentioned, along with "his auld baird gray" (147–48), the latter possibly referring to the name of a horse.

1718   Gilbert of the White Hand, called Robin Hood's equal in archery in the late fifteenth-century *A Geste of Robyn Hode* (stanzas 292, 401).

1719   The Hays of Naughton were a branch of the noble Hay family; *Madin land* is the name given to the land of the Amazons in *Mandeville's Travels* (83).

1720   Marginal note in L: *Nigramansye*. *Nigramansy* is a type of performance which depends more on machinery than on gesture for the creation of illusion; it was in vogue at the court of James IV, its most noted practitioner being Andrew Forman, Bishop of Moray (Baxter 167–68).

1721   B tentatively identifies *Bonitas* as Guido Bonatus de Forlivio, thirteenth-century astrologer and supposed magician whose treatises circulated widely during the fifteenth century (Thorndike 2.827, 839); Roger Bacon, a thirteenth-century Franciscan friar who became (along with Friar Bungay) "in popular tradition a nigromancer, conjurer, and magician" (Thorndike 2.680).

1722–28 These examples of *juglory* (tricks of illusion and transformation by sleight of hand; *DOST juglery*) parallel those in *The House of Fame* 1259–81 and *The Buke of the Howlat* 770–93.

1724	B cites the use of *singing bone* to refer to the "funny bone" (*OED singing,* 4).
1730	"Pastime and games" is the category for the various performances listed in the three previous stanzas, not the whole preceding catalogue of heroes.
1737	The silliness and cowardice of sheep are proverbial (Whiting S213, 204).
1746	Compare this assertion of readiness with the dreamer's subsequent hesitation (1757).
1756	Marginal note in L: *By thys boke he menis Virgil*; this assignment recalls the task Alceste sets for Chaucer (*The Legend of Good Women* F prologue 479–91) with one difference: whereas Alceste tells Chaucer what to write, Venus shows Douglas the book he will write (Morse 112).
1761	Marginal note in L: *The Auctors conclution of Venus merour*; this contradicts the poem, in which the "conclusion" (which does not offer an accurate description of the catalogue just finished) is the Nymph's.
1767	Marginal note in L: *The Palice of honour is patent for honest vertuus men an[d] not for vicius fals & craftye pepyll.*
1772	Cicero's book consists of his four speeches denouncing Catiline to the Senate of Rome (*Against Catiline*). These speeches (and especially the first) became models of invective oration.
1775	On Jugurtha, see note for 1688–89; the usurper Tryphon murdered Antiochus Epiphanes and Jonathas Maccabeus, only to be deposed (1 Maccabees 13:20–32, 14:1, 15:25–39).
1780	Marginal note in L: *Falsehed the moder of al vice.*
1785–88	Compare the two sorts of failure (idleness and faithlessness) shown in the fiery gulf (1315–83).
1790	Marginal note in L: *Patience.*
1792–1827	Allegorizing the officers of the royal court is a convention of fifteenth-century dream visions (*King Hart* 301–08; *Court of Sapience* 1471–1652).

1792–1824   Marginal note in L: *The discriptio[n] of the Prince of hie honore wyth hys Palys & Court. Charity Constance. Liberalite Innocens devocyon Humanite Trew relation pease temperance. Humilite. discypline mercye Conscience justyse prudence diligens clene lyvyng. Hope. Piety. Fortitud, Veryte.*

1798, 1801   At the Scottish court, the treasurer received royal revenue from feudal duties, fines, and special taxes; the comptroller administered royal revenue from rents, leases, and customs duties (Nicholson 566–67, 570).

1800   The clerk of closet and the cubicular were attendants to the king in his bedchamber, the first his private confessor, the second his groom or personal servant.

1806   The Cardinal Virtue of Temperance.

1807   Humility is the quality revealed by Chaucer's Squire in his carving at table for his father (*CT* 1.99–100).

1810–11   The Chancellor of a Scottish court "presided over the king's parliaments and councils and kept the king's great seal, the most solemn means of authenticating documents drawn up in chancery — the royal secretariat" (Nicholson 22); Conscience similarly refuses to let Meed sway his judgment in *Piers Plowman* Passus 3 (Passus 4 of C-text).

1814   The *-ing* suffix indicates the infinitive form of the verb here; the line in L is no less typical of Douglas and metrically correct than that in E (see B).

1816   The audit of the royal accounts was an annual affair performed by the Lords Auditours of the Exchequer, officers specially appointed for this duty (Nicholson 22–23).

1818   The outstewarts are managers of Crown lands (Nicholson 380).

1821   The almoner, a cleric connected with the royal chapel, responsible for the collection and distribution of the King's alms (Mertes, p. 50).

1834–36   Golden doors decorated with scenes (of military triumph not natural phenomena) open upon the shrine of Caesar in Virgil's *Georgics* (3.25–39); a closer parallel exists in Ovid's description of the silver doors of the palace of the Sun (*Metamorphoses* 2.3–20); Douglas is "[guided], perhaps, by allegorical interpretations of Ovid's *Metamorphoses* in which Helios was allegorised as God, and the throne of Helios as the Throne of Glory" (Norton-Smith 249).

1837	Ovid's description also begins with the depiction on the doors of the earth surrounded by the seas (2.5–6). The passage of the poet's lofty view as he looks down upon earth echoes Geoffrey's flight on the talons of the eagle in *The House of Fame*, and also Troilus's view of earth in the epilogue to *Troilus and Criseyde*.
1839	Water and earth are the other two elements.
1840–45	Douglas writes a similar catalogue of astronomical terms in *Eneados* 8. prol. 149–53.
1840	The seven spheres are the courses of the seven planets (Saturn, Jupiter, Mars, Venus, Mercury, the sun, and the moon) revolving around the earth according to the Ptolemaic system; the *primum mobile,* the source of planetary motion, is the outermost sphere moving on an axis, at either end of which are the Pole Stars (see note to lines 1843–44).
1841	Marginal note in L: *Astronami*. The signs of the twelve astrological houses on the zodiac are Aries, Taurus, Gemini, Cancer, Leo, Virgo, Libra, Sagittarius, Scorpio, Capricorn, Aquarius, and Pisces.
1842	"*Zodiacus* is a cercle that passith aslont and is departid evene in twelve parties, the which xii parties philosophris clepith signes; and thise signes schewith to us what partie of heven the sonne and the planetis beth inne" (*On the Properties of Things* 1.460 [8.9]).
1843–44	The Pole Stars, *arcticus* being the one which "alway schineth to us and never gooth doun to oure sight, for alwey he is above us," and *antarcticus*, "the southeren sterre," which "is alwey unseyn to us" (*On the Properties of Things* 1.501 [8.22]); these two stars mark the uppermost and downmost points of "the spere of heven" on which the stars are fixed (1.457 [8.6]).
1844–45	Ursa Major and Ursa Minor, the constellations known in North America as the Big Dipper and Little Dipper; the *sevyn sterris* are the Pleiades;

Phaethon (according to Ovid, *Metamorphoses* 2.317–20) may be taken to be a shooting star or meteor, like the *impressioun* which shocks the dreamer at the outset of the poem (105), or it may be an epithet for the sun (Norton-Smith 253); the *Charle wane* is another name for Ursa Major.

1846–48   Ovid tells the story of the abduction of Ganymede in *Metamorphoses* 10.155–61; Douglas's allusion to this tale of divine lust contrasts with Douglas's previous emphasis on the moral worth of the officers at the court of Honour (1783–1827); as the only human being depicted on the gate, "Ganymede may represent the poet and other literary figures who were privileged to go on a celestial voyage in order to receive superior instruction about some Universal" (Norton-Smith 249).

1849–54   This passage is a fairly close translation of *Metamorphoses* 2.11–14, except that there the sea-nymphs have green hair and ride on fishes as well as swim.

1855–59   Similar lists of terms of astronomy occur in Henryson, *Fables* 628–41, and *Court of Sapience* 2108–70.

1856   In Ptolemaic astronomy, each of the seven planets was supposed to revolve on its own orbit (or *epicycle*) around the earth, but also to move along a greater circle (the *deferent*); opposition has occurred when two planets are exactly opposite to each other from the perspective of the earth, or when a planet is opposite to the sun ("it is a signe of parfite emnyte and bodeth worst happis, and namliche yif Mars hath soche aspecte to Saturnus othir to the sonne"; *On the Properties of Things* 1.465 [8.9]).

1857   In Ptolemaic astronomy, three kinds of planetary motion are distinguished: direct, stationary, and retrograde (*On the Properties of Things* 1.477–78 [8.11]).

1858   A planet's natural motion is its revolution in its sphere; its daily motion is its diurnal course across the sky in relation to a point on the zodiac (*On the Properties of Things* 1.476–77 [8.11]).

1859   *Aspect* is the position of a planet on the zodiac relative to another planet from the vantage point of the earth; *digression* is the apparent deviation in the courses of the "inferior planets" Venus and Mercury.

1862–63   This passage concludes where Douglas's source had begun, with the assertion that the artistry of the depictions exceeded the value of the material from which they were made (*Metamorphoses* 2.5).

1865   Norton-Smith compares this with the impatient shove Africanus gives the erring dreamer in Chaucer's *Parliament of Fowls* (153–54).

1866–68   "What devil" is a common expletive phrase *(MED s.v. devil; DOST s.v. devil*); for all its raciness of style, the Nymph's scolding may recall the Sibyl's rebuke of Aeneas for staring overlong at the depictions on the doors to Daedalus' temple of Apollo (*Aeneid* 6.37–39; Norton-Smith 249).

1878   The empyrean is the highest heaven, above the moving spheres; it is the home of the angels and the "contrey and wonynge of blisful men" (*On the Properties of Things* 1.454 [8.4]); whether or not he is to be taken as the Christian God, Honour lives in a place *like* Heaven; compare Lindsay, *Dream*, lines 514–18 (*Works* I.19).

1879–80   The tall tree and the low shrub are traditional emblems for high and low style (Curtius 201 n.; Norton-Smith 247).

1891   The *breddyt* doors and windows are shuttered, not boarded up: his view thus obstructed, the dreamer "must view the interior of the palace in a single, circumscribed peep" (Norton-Smith 253).

1898   By *knots* Douglas is referring to ornamental patterns of interlace, worked in gold and enamel upon the ivory; a *devyse* is an emblematic design inscribed with a motto.

1902   Topaz "schyneth most whan he is ysmyte with the sonne beeme, and passeth in clerenesse alle othere precious stones, and comforteth men and bestes to beholde and loke theronne. . . . And in tresorie of kynges nothing is more cleere ne more precious than this precious stone" (*On the Properties of Things* 2.877–78 [16.95]).

1903   The *boir* is a chink in the shutters on the door; see note to line 1891.

1913   Sapphire "hath vertue to reule and acorde hem that bene in stryf and helpeth moche to make pees and acorde"; in ancient times it was "singulerliche yhalowed to Appolyn" (*On the Properties of Things* 2.869–70 [16.86]).

1921   *Armypotent* is an epithet for Mars (*CT* 1.1124; Lydgate, *Troy Book* prologue 4; Lindsay, *The Historie of Squyer Meldrum*, line 390 [*Works* I.156] and *The Testament of Squyer Meldrum*, line 76 [*Works* I.190]. Compare Douglas' *Aeneid* 2.425, 6.839, 9.717). In its place in E appears the explicitly Christian term *omnipotent*, on which interpretations of the poem have hinged (Lewis 290; Spearing *Dream* 210–11; Kratzmann 117–19). E's reading might be taken as a Protestant editor's attempt to resolve Douglas's balance of pagan and Christian towards the latter at this crucial point, a resolution arguably present in E's weak substitution of *Verteouslie* for L's *Victoriusly* (1966; compare *vertuus*, 1964). If L's "Chaucerian adjective is the right reading, then perhaps the Mars-like figure on the throne is an oblique reference to King James" (Norton-Smith 252–53). To be sure, Mars has not previously been sighted in the Palace (1471); but Douglas's God of Honor also deserves comparison with Ovid's Sun-god (see note to lines 1834–36) and Chaucer's God of Love (see note following).

1922–24   With his brightness of face, this god recalls Chaucer's God of Love, whose hair is crowned with a sun: "Therwith me thoghte his face shoon so bryghte / That wel unnethes myghte I him beholde" (*The Legend of Good Women* F prol. 232–33); see also 1948–51; see also Henryson's lines on Apollo: "The brichtnes of his face quhen it was bair / Nane micht behald for peirsing of his sicht" (*Testament* 206–07).

1942   *Carling* (the feminine equivalent of "churl") is a common term of abuse in colloquial Older Scots (*DOST carling*).

1944   A cynically anticlerical jibe; having a common-law wife was not an unusual circumstance for a late-medieval priest, and was a topic of satire well before the Reformation (Dowden, pp. 309–19).

1946   Colloquial style accounts for the obscurity of the first word: in L, the adverb *Langere* ("longer") may be read as a terse, disjunctive version of "Had you remained unconscious any longer," and, later in the line, *had* is a compressed version of the past subjunctive ("you would have had"; Aitken, "Variational Variety," pp. 176–209). Less convincingly if more explicitly, E's version of the first word (*Lang eir,* "long before") implies that the Nymph's fears for the dreamer were aroused (and allayed) some time before he regained consciousness.

1953   L's reading *malt* appears to be the past tense of the verb *melt,* which is ungrammatical here; it may, however, be a corruption of the original reading, referring to the feebleness of the dreamer's heart (*DOST melt,* with *meltit, melted, meltyn* as usual forms of the past participle; *MED melte,* 1b, 2b); compare *Pearl* 1154: "My maneʒ mynde to maddyng malte."

1957   Referring to the court of the Muse Calliope.

1978–94   A summary of various traditional expressions about the transcience of earthly glory, conventional images included being the dream (1983; see Whiting L241), the sunbeam (1987), and the weltering sea (1989; see 1349–55; Whiting S113, 107); the passage ends with a catalogue of the powerful of church and state, all under the term of Death (Tristram 169–74; Woolf 325, 343–47).

1995   The doctrine of Good Works is best known through the moral play *Everyman* (906–07); see further 2013–15.

2000   Marginal note in L: *A comendacion of vertue quhilk is the vay to honour and not riches or hie blud.*

2019   Marginal note in L: *Exemplis of vertuus men and women.* The Nine Nobles are Joshua, David, Judas Maccabeus, Hector, Alexander, Julius Caesar, Arthur, Charlemagne, and Godfrey of Boulogne (Christian hero of the First Crusade).

2024   Semiramis, Assyrian queen, whom Gower calls a whore (*Confessio Amantis* 5.1432–33), and Chaucer a wicked *virago* (*CT* 2.359; see also *Fall of Princes* 1.6632–43), but who is also famed for building a wall around Babylon (*The Legend of Good Women* 707), and is called "Most generous gem and floure of lovely favor" and "a mighty conqueror" in the Chaucerian poem "The Nine Ladies Worthy" (Utley 224–25); Tomyris, Scythian queen, vanquisher of Cyrus of Persia, of whose victory Lydgate says, "It is an horrour in maner for to thynke / So gret a prynce rebuked for to be / Off a woman" (*Fall of Princes* 2.3893–94), and who, together with Semiramis and others, is praised in the fifteenth-century English translation of Boccaccio's *De claris mulieribus (Concerning Illustrious Women;* Utley 219); Hippolyta, Amazon queen, defeated by Theseus (see lines 1195–96), praised in the aforementioned "Nine Ladies."

2025 Penthesileia (see line 341, note); although E's *Medea* may seem a likelier reading than L's *Medus,* L may be correct, Medusa having started off as "a creature in fayrenes above nature" who had "the most cunnynge in knowynge the tyllynge and plantynge of trees," and who was turned into a monster because she polluted the temple of Minerva (Boccaccio, *De Claris Mulieribus* 70–71); Xenobia, queen of Palmyra and conqueror of the eastern provinces of the Roman Empire, defeated by the Emperor Aurelian (The Monk's Tale, *CT* 7.2247–2734).

2027 Grig (Latinized by the fourteenth-century Scottish chronicler John of Fordun as Gregorius; 1.159–61, 2.149–52), king of Scots (878–89), reputedly victorious in Ireland and northern England; Kenneth Mac Alpin (reigned 843–50), who unified the kingdoms of the Picts and the Scots into one kingdom; Robert Bruce (king of Scots 1306–29), restorer of the independence of Scotland from England, and hero of John Barbour's epic *Brus.*

2031–43 Marginal note in L: *Vicious people punyshed. Invye Pride, Ignorance, Disseyt.*

2035–46 The displacement of sons of gentle birth by churlish upstarts and the corruption of morals among the nobility are topics of Dunbar's court satires ("This waverand warldis wretchidnes," 29–52; "Schir, yit remember," 11–25; "Complane I wald, wist I quhome till," 15–38; "Into this warld may none assure," 21–30).

2044 Marginal note in L: *Dissate & craftynes ar haldyn wisdome now a dayes. verite & justice is callyt simplycitye & folyshnes.*

2064 See note to 1879.

2068–76 Concerning trees that grow gems and barnacle geese reputed to be generated out of sodden driftwood or living trees, see Alexander Neckam's *De naturis rerum* and *Mandeville's Travels.* Such tales circulated widely as folklore in eastern Scotland in the late fifteenth century (Brown *Travellers* 26, 56–57; *Documents* 89–91, 155–56).

2089   As B notes, "such shock-awakenings are common in medieval dream poems" (*The Parliament of Fowls* 693–95; Dunbar's *Goldyn Targe* 238–46, "Thrissill and the Rois" 183–84, "Ane Dreme" 111–15, and "Fenyeit Freir" 125–26). Sometimes the shock involves entering water, as in *Pearl* 1157–70.

2090   Marginal note in L: *The aucthour returnes frome his dreame to him self agane.*

2106   *fund.* ME *finden* has a wealth of meanings, ranging from "to discover," "find," "ascertain," "judge" to "compose," "invent," "counterfeit," or "tell" (see MED's twenty-three separate entries, each with several shades of meaning). When the dreamer awakens in Chaucer's *The Book of the Duchess* he will "fonde to put this swevene in ryme" (1332; n.b. Chaucer's punning on the word in 1325, 1329). Here Douglas's dreamer yearns to remain in the country of poetic invention that he "fund" (found, invented) in his dream.

2116   Marginal note in L: *A ballade in the commendation of honour & verteu.*

2116–42   Internal rhyme is a technique of closure in Older Scots verse (Henryson, "Ane Prayer for the Pest," 65–88; Dunbar, "The Flyting of Dunbar and Kennedie" 233–48, 545–52, David Lindsay's *Testament of the Papyngo* 1179–85; also Dunbar's "Ballat of Our Lady" throughout); B notes that "the imagery has religious associations, several of the figures being traditionally applied to Christ or the Virgin; and Douglas frequently addresses Honour as if he were addressing God."

2150   The admission that one's work is rustic and crude is part of a traditional rhetorical strategy of affected modesty; usually, however, it occurs at the outset of a work (Curtius 411; *CT* 5.716–20).

2161–69   This is an amplification of the humility of Chaucer's envoy to *Troilus and Criseyde* (5.1786–92); see also *The Kingis Quair* 1352–65 and *Goldyn Targe* 271–79.

2167   *stouth.* B glosses *stouth* as a variant of *stulth*, "theft" (ON *stuldar;* compare *stealth),* the sense of this line belittling the poet's book thus being: "Thow art but pilfered materials. Theft loves light but little." But Douglas may be punning. *Stouth* is a legal term for "a customary rent" (*MED stuth* sb) which seems a fitting sense given the reference to *quytcleme* in the previous line. According to this reading Douglas says he has paid his dues by writing this poem, albeit small payment, "not worth a myte."

Textual Notes

In collation, variants in the suffix to the third person singular present form of the verb (*ith/is*) and in the present-participial suffix (*and/ing*) are not recorded. Likewise, variation in medial vowel is not recorded (compare L's *quhame* and E's *quhome*; also *so* versus *sa*). L does not present a thoroughly anglicized text of the poem: *quh-* regularly appears for *wh-*, for instance; and frequently L contains older forms of the Scots words found in E (e.g., *till* for *to*; *a* for *ane*; *not* for *nocht*; *ald* for *auld*; *perist* for *perischit*).

Rubric above 1 The Prologue] E; *om.* L   **3** *be]* L; *the* E   **21** *Above]* L D; *Abone* E   **25** *eccon]* L D; echo E   **39** preserve] L D; reserve E   **57** stone] E D; stune L   **88** auchtyst] L; auchtis E   **99** puncys] L; pulsis E   **101** dasyt] L D; desie E   vary] E; veray L   **109** dasyt] L; desyit E   **111** hetis] L D; heiring E   **Rubric above 127** The First Part] E; *om.* L   **132** ranys] L; rymis E   **134** their] L; thir E   **144** skauppis] L D; swappis E   **148** monsturis] D; monstruis L; monstures E   **157** royk] L; rock E   **186** suythly] L; surelie E   **213** four] L; all E   **220** rayed] L; raid E   **284** overwhort] L; overthort E   **302** syse] E; lyse L   **320** syng] L; signe E   **360-1** [order of lines reversed from that in L and E]   **361** soundis] L; sounding E   **363** caryit] E; carit L   **372** Inoth] L; Inwith E   **379** inoth] L; inwith E   **385** tofore] L; befoir E   and] L; or E   **388** Lang ere]; Langere L; Langer E   **436** thair] L; thir E   **444** ordours] E; ordour L   **462** than] L; nor E   **472** wondryt] L; wonder E   **486** yit] E; yf L   **497** songin] L; soung E   **510** kyng] L; *om.* E   **514** igroundit] E; groundit L   **518** gekgo] L; greik E   **534** of brounvert] or brounvert L; ovirbrouderit E   **540** velvot] E; velvos L   **576** France] E; Fare L   **591** fyrm] L; *om.* E   **613** involupit] E; involvit L   syte] E; dispyte L   **617** fait] L; fact E   **644** in greif] L; and greit E   **663** pane full] L; panefull E   **666** accusyng] L; accusen E   of] E; as of L   **698** am and aucht] E; am aucht L   **719** distrublys] L; disturbis E   **737** die] E; be L   **740** transfigurat] E; transfigurit L   **742** mischaip] E; myssape L   **752** quhow] L; how E   **772** Lo] L; To E   **775** quhilk that] L; that quhilk E   **786** lusty] L; luik E   **805** *om.* E   **806** held the measure] E; held mesure L   **817** thair layis] L; thay ladyis E   **818** na way compere] L; na compeir E   **825** in] L; into E   gastly] L; greit E   **826** now] L; new E   **827** thair] E; the L   **831** knawledge] E; knawlagis L   **833** our mate] L; or meit E   **836** polit] L; poet E   sang] L; singand E   **843** lede all of] L; leid of E   **852** Thespis the mothyr] L; Thespis mother E   of the Musis] E; of musis L   **859** cronikillis] L; chronikill E   **865** play] L; *om.* E   **869** and sistir schene] L; sister with croun E   **872** that] L; the E   **882** Phanee] L; fair E   **883** Dryades Saturee] L; Dryades and Saturee

E **886** dempt] L; demit E **888** afore] L; befoir E **890** tofore] L; befoir E **910** of the vale] E; of Vale L **914** clerkis] L; clerk E **932** standand] E; standan L **933** the] L; my E **934** sammyn thir] L; thir samin E **939** langer] L; lang E **942** wes the cause] L; was caus E thair of hir] L; of hir thair E **946** hes] L; had E **948** dispitefull subtelle] L; dispitefull and subtell E **949** on] L; and E **950** wallaway] L; velanie E **951** my] L; our E **954** rebell] L; rebald E **959** All out than wes his sclander or sich plede] L; To sic as he to mak conterpleid E **960** renoun] L; honour E **961** your fame so wyd] L; sa wide your fame E **968** this] L; his E **966** oft] L; efter E **971** afore] L; befoir E **975** afore] L; befoir E **984** No woman is rather a] L; A vennom is rather and a E **986** inequyte] L; iniquitie E **990** serve] L; have E **1004** releschit] L; relevit E **1016** preservit] L; deliverit E **1022** lait and air] L; but dispair E **1024** thou in joy and plesour may repair] L; In lestand blis to remane and repair **1026** peace] L; pietie E **1029** and] L; or E **1034** now be] L; thow be E **1037** purifyit] L; perfite E **1040** gard] L; guerdoun E **1043** *om.* E **1044** of dangare] L; of all dangeir E **1048** campion] L; companioun E **1052** In ane instant] E; In instant L **1053** thir] E; hir L **1087** Almane] L; Almanie E **1088** in Ytalie] L; into Italie E **1090** The montayns] L; The hie montanes E of all Garmanie] L; of Germanie E **1092** Tiber] E; Tirbir L **1143** never] L; not E **1144** hors] L; horsis E **1150** sterny] L; stannerie E **1176** musis] L; ladyis E **1177** deace] L; deissis E **1191** fetis] L; fatis E **1194** to the deith] E; to deth L **1195** tald] L; schew E **1213** nor] L; or E **1218** hondris] L; hundrethis E **1224** in] L; of E **1231** or] L; and E **1253** rydyng] L; ryden E **1280** rememorance] L; remembrance E **1301** as] L; to E **1302** Ascens] L; The ascence E **1309** mismaid] L; dismaid E **1313** we] L; I E **1327** nene] L; na E **1331** se] L; be E **1334** pieteous]E; pituis L **1338** drynt] L; drownit E **1354** palyce] L; place E folk to] L; folk for to E **1363** boldyn] L; bairdin E **1365** schip] L; schipis E **1367** the] L; swa E **1368** tobryst] L; did brist E **1373** firre and] L; fir tre and E **1376** drynt and part] L; drownit part E **1379** tha] L; that E **1380** drint] L; drownit E **1399** endytyng] L; endyten E **1403** salt thou] L; thow sall E **1409** transcendes sa far] L; transcendis far E **1415** every] L; alkyn E **1423** thyng] L; things E **1424** fare] L; sair E **1427** impossybill] L; unpossibill E **1428** of] L; with E **1431** fanys] L; thanis E **1437** jalmys] L; jalme E **1440** Tofore] L; Befoir E **1460** a] E; *om.* L **1464** eftirwartis] L; efterwart E **1472** afore] L; befoir E **1473** Twelf amarant stagis stude] L; Stude emeraut stages E **1475** Sustenttand] L; Upstandand E aforne] L; beforne E **1482** uthir] L; utter E **1484** wound] L; woundit E **1487** purifyed precius] L; purifyit and precious E **1492** subtil quent spectacle] L; subtell spectakill E **1494** ful] L; *om.* E **1498** creacion] L; creatiounis E **1506** Twelf] L; Ten E **1513** In] L; Of E **1528** douchty] L; michtie E **1555** chyldir] L; children E **1569** the] L; this E **1572** tyrrand lyk all Jowrye he] L; tyranlie he Jowrie all E **1573** mony knychtly] L; mony ane knichtlie E **1581** Wes distroyit] L; Destroyit was E **1589** thiddir] L; hidder E **1599**

of] L; in E   **1602** the] L; that E   **1605** that] L; thair E   **1607** to] L; at E   **1616** navyn]
L; navie E   **1617** thousand] E; thosand L   **1653** huge] L; greit E   **1667** Atwene] L;
Betwene E   **1670** Atwene] L; Betwene E   **1676** Marcus Curtius] E; Quincyus L   **1677**
the] E; *om.* L   **1680** enarmyt]; onarmyt L; unarmit E   **1692** atwine] L; betwene E
1705 Newand] E; Mewand L   **1711-19** *om.* L   **1720** I] E; *om.* L   **1726** parys] L;
paroche E   a small penny] L; ane penny E   **1736** that] L; this E   **1740** I] L; scho E
1748 bousum]; bousoum L; bowsum E   **1758** tho] L; scho E   **1783** The garatour my
Nymphe tho to] L; That garitour tho my nimphe unto E   **1784** the] L; that E   **1794**
disservys] L; dois serve E   **1795** gudlines the flour] E; gudlynes is the flour L   **1803**
morow and eve] L; morne and evin E   **1804** wakis] L; walkis E   **1807** lyst greve] L; list
to greif E   **1811** pronounce fals] E; pronounce a fals L   **1814** lyst committing] L; listin
commit E   **1816** ovirseis] L; ovirse E   **1835** thair was] E; thair of L   **1850** Dorida] L;
Driada E   **1856** episciclis] L; epistillis E   opposionis] L; oppositiounis E   **1857**
porturyt] L; portrait E   **1859** Eclipse] L; Eclipsis E   **1860** I mony] L; I and mony E
1884 Swa] E; Fra L   **1886** soithly] soithla L surelie E   me] E; my L   **1890** paithit] L;
pachit E   **1898** sle] L; hie E   **1899** wes] L; war E   **1908** ne] L; not E   **1921**
armypotent] L; omnipotent E   **1924** byrsyt] L; brissit E   **1933** my] L; that E   **1938** is]
L; was E   **1942** at] L; that E   **1946** Langere] L; Lang eir E   ne] L; nor E   **1953** malt]
L; mad E   **1954** quod scho na mare] L; na mair quod scho E   **1956** suythly] L; surelie
E   **1960** postrum] L; posterne E   **1961** passage] E; passagis L   **1962** the] L; that E
1966 Victoriusly] L; Verteouslie E   **1968** mane] E; name L   **1972** ryng] L; king E
1973 honoring] L; governing E   **1981** warldly glore] L; warldis glorie E   **1985** tofore]
L; befoir E   **2001** ma] L; can E   **2009** honour lestand] L; lestand honour E   **2022** ma]
E; may L   **2025** Medus] L; Medea E   **2038** selvyn] L; selfis E   **2074** swomand] L;
swemand E   **2077** the] E; thay L   **2082** passagis] L; passage E   **2097** swounyt] L;
swemit E   **2105** In purpose] L; I purpoisit E   **2118** renoun] L; honour E   **2129** myche]
L; mekill E   **2149** the] L; *om.* E

Glossary

[This list contains only those hard words which occur more than once in the poem. When *y* is used as a vowel, it is considered equivalent to *i*.]

abaisit (p.p.) *abashed, confused, embarrassed*

abaid (p.t. of **abide**) *waited, lingered*

accion, actioun (n.) *legal suit*

affray (n.) *fear, alarm*

affray (v.) *frighten* (**affrayit**, p.p.)

afore (prep., adv.) *before*

ay (adv.) *always, continually*

ale (v.) *trouble, distress; be harmed* (**alyt**, p.t.)

air, ayrly (adv.) *early*

alkyn (adj.) *every kind of*

alanerly (adv.) *only, just*

als (adv.) *also* (**als . . . as**, *as . . . as*)

alswyith, als swyth (adv.) *immediately*

ameis (v.) *soothe*

ane (indef. art.) *a(n);* (adj.) *one*

anewch, eneuch (adv.) *enough*

arrasyt (p.p.) *uprooted, pulled away*

art (n.) *district*

at (rel. pron.) *that*

athir (adj.) *either*

at rychtis, at ryght (adv.) *suitably, excellently*

atwene, atwine (prep.) *between*

avayle, avale (n.) *value, reputation*

aucht (v.) *ought* (**auchtyst**, second pers. sing.)

awalk (v.) *awaken* (**awolk**, p.t.)

bair (n.) *boar*

ballat (n.) *song, lyric poem* (**ballattis**, pl.)

be (prep.) *with, by means of, by*

bedene (adv.) *completely, straightaway*

behest (n.) *command*

beild (v.) *build* (**beildit**, p.t., p.p.)

beis (**be**, pres. 3rd pers. sing. and pl.) *must be, is (are)*

belive (adv.) *quickly*

bene (**be**, pres. 3rd pers. pl.) *are*

benyng (adj.) *benevolent, gracious*

bent (n.) *field*

beriall, byrriall (n.) *beryl*

betaucht (p.t., p.p.) *entrusted, consigned*

betrais (v.) *betray* (**betrasyt**, p.p.)

bysnyng (n., adj.) *monster; ill-omened*

blaw (v.) *blow* (**blawyn, blaw**, p.p.) *broadcast, published*

blenk (n., v.) *glance* (**blent**, p.t.)

blomed (p.p.) *blossoming, covered with flowers*

bot, but (prep.) *without*

bot gyf (conj.) *unless*

bousum (adj.) *obedient, willing*

breid (n.) *breadth*
brevyt (p.p.) *written, recorded*
brukkylnes (n.) *instability, frailty*
bustuus (adj.) *rough*
but let (adv.) *immediately, unhindered*

castis (pl. n.) *devices of rhetoric*
catyve (n.) *wretch, miserable* or *worthless person, captive*
chaire, chare (n.) *chariot*
cheis (v.) *choose* (cheisit, p.p.)
circumstance (n.) *ceremoniousness; detail*
claithis (n.) *clothes*
clepys (v., 3rd pers.) *calls* (clepit, p.p.)
close (n.) *courtyard*
clois (v.) *encircle* (closyd, p.t. *fastened*)
commovyt (v., p.t. and p.p.) *aroused, annoyed*
compere (n.) *rival, equal*
condyng (adj.) *fitting, worthy*
consave (v.) *perceive, understand*
convoy (v.) *accompany, guide* (convoyit, p.p.)
cure (n.) *attention, care, task*

dant (v.) *subdue*
degest (adj.) *dignified, calm*
deid (n.) *death*
deir, dere (v.) *disturb, injure*
demand (n.) *objection, counter-argument*
deming (infinitive of v. deme) *judge*
den (n.) *a deep, narrow valley*
dere (adj.) *precious*
deservis, disservys (3rd pers. sing. of v. deserve) *serves*
devail (v.) *lower* (devalys, 3rd pers. sing.)

devyse (n.) *design;* at device *according to plan*
diffyne (v.) *describe*
do (v.) *take, cause*
drynt (p.p.) *drowned*
dulce (adj.) *sweet*

e (n.) *eye* (eyn, pl.)
effere (n.) *manner*
eik (adv.) *also*
enbroude (p.p.) *stained, dyed*
endyt, endyte (n.) *literary style*
endyte, indyte (v.) *compose*
enforcis (v., 3rd pers. sing.) *exerts*
engreve (v.) *annoy* (engrevit, p.t.)
entalyeit, entailyeit (p.p.) *sculpted, formed*
erdly (adj.) *earthly*
eschevyt (p.p.) *emerged*
evyr (n.) *ivory*
expremit, expremyt (p.p.) *described*
expres (adv.) *precisely*

facund (adj.) *eloquent, giving eloquence*
fare (v.) *travel*
fate (n.) *deed* (feitis, pl.) *practices*
fary (n.) *daze*
fede (n.) *hostility*
feil, fele (adj.) *many, great*
ferdnes (n.) *fear*
fel, fell (adj.) *fierce*
fere (n.) *companions, company* (see also in fere)
ferly, ferlye (n.) *wonder;* farlyes (pl.) *marvels*
flete (v.) *flow;* flet (p.t.) *float*
flewer, flewour (n.) *scent*

flud, flude (n.) *river, flood* (**fludis**, pl.)

forvay (v.) *go astray* (**forvayt**, p.t.)

fra (conj.) *once, when*

frane (v.) *ask* (**franyt**, p.t.)

freuch (adj.) *frail, ephemeral*

fulfyllet, fulfillyt (p.p.) *well-stocked, abounding*

gate (n.) *way, ambush*

gam, game (n.) *merriment, contest*;

gemmys (pl.) *recreations*

gang (v.) *walk*

gar (v.) *cause* (**garrys**, 3rd pers. sing.; **gart**, p.t.)

garth (n.) *enclosed garden, yard*

gyf (see **bot gyf**)

glance (n.) *flash, gleam* (**glancis**, pl.)

godly (adj.) *divine*

gre (n.) *degree* (**greis**, pl.) *levels, steps*

greif (n.) *displeasure, anger, spite*

gryis, gryse (v.) *(cause to) shudder*

guerdoun, gwardoun (n.) *reward*

hail, hale (adj.) *healthy, whole*

hail (adv.) *wholly*

hailsum, halsom (adj.) *healthful*

hald, halde (n.) *abode, stronghold*

havinges, havyngis (pl. n.) *manners*

hecht, heycht (v.) *is called*

heir (v.) *hear*

hes (v.) *has*

hie (adj.) *high*

hycht (n.) *summit, exaltation*

hyng (v.) *hang* (**hyngis**, 3rd pers. pl.; **hang**, p.t.)

hynt (v., p.t.) *seized, took*

ygroundyt (p.p.) *trained*

ilk (adj.) *same, each*

imprent (v.) *impart, retain* (**imprentis**, 3rd pers. sing.)

indyte (see **endyte**)

in fere (adv. phrase) *together*

ingrave (p.p.) *engraved, cut*

ingres (n.) *entry*

inoth (prep.) *within*

in tyl (prep.) *within, into*

iwys (adv.) *indeed*

jape (n.) *prank, trick*

justefy (v.) *pass judgment upon*

ken (v.) *know* (**kend**, p.t., p.p.)

kyith, kyth (v.) *recognize, show*

layf, lave (n.) *remainder*

laythly (adj.) *loathsome*

lare (n.) *learning, teaching*

lang ere (adv.) *a while ago*

law (adj.) *low*

lawte (n.) *loyalty*

leyl, lele (adj.) *loyal*

lestand (pres. part.) *lasting*

let (see **but let**)

list (v.) *wish*

lufsum, lusum (adj.) *lovely*

lusty (adj.) *fresh, vigorous, "fine"*

maid (v.) *made*

maket (v.) *made*

mal eys (n. phrase) *discomfort, distress*

mane (n.) *strength*

mate (n.) *companion*

meyne, mene (v.) *mean, declare*

mekill (adj.) *great* (adv.) *greatly*

me thynk (impers.) *it seems to me* (**me**

thocht, p.t.)
micht (n.) *might*
mych, myche (adj.) *much*
mysmaid (p.p.) *upset, troubled*
myte (n.) *the smallest, least valuable coin*
mo (adj., pron.) *more*
mot (v.) *may*
mow (n.) *joke, quip*
muskan, muskane (adj.) *rotten*

not (pron.) *nothing*
not (v.) *know not*

on (prep.) *in*
onabysitly (adv.) *boldly*
on raw (adv. tag) *all together*
or (conj.) *before*
ovyrset (v., p.t. and p.p.) *overwhelmed, overturned*

pycht (p.p.) *pitched, set*
pyne (n.) *pain, punishment*
plane (adj.) *flat, open*
plede, pleid (n.) *dispute, protest*
plenyeit (p.t.) *complained*
port (n.) *gate*
preve (v.) *test*
pres (n.) *crowd*
pretend (v.) *intend, presume, profess*
proces (n.) *proceedings, discourse*

quent (adj.) *elegant, intricate*
quha (pron.) *who*
quhair, quhare (adv.) *where*
quham, quhom (pron.) *that, whom*
quhat (pron.) *what*
quhen (adv.) *when*

quhy (adv.) *why*
quhilk, quhilkis (pron.) *which*
quhill (conj.) *until, while*
quhilum (adv.) *formerly*
quyk, quyke (adj.) *lifelike*
quhite (adj.) *white*
quhois (adj.) *whose*
quod (v., p.t.) *said*
quuke (v., p.t.) *trembled*
quhois (pron.) *whose*

raid (p.t.) *rode*
ravyst (p.p.) *"ravished," abducted*
raw (see on raw)
recomfort, reconfort (v., p.t. and p.p.) *refreshed*
rede, reid (n.) *counsel*
relatioun (n.) *report*; **relationys** (pl.) *discourses*
remane (v.) *dwell* (**remanyt**, p.t.)
remede, remeid (n.) *remedy, redress*
repair (v.) *dwell*
represent (n.) *scene, appearance* (**representis**, pl.)
rethoreis, rethoryis (n., pl.) *rhetoricians*
richt, right (adv.) *very, exactly*
rychtis, ryght (see at rychtis)
rydyng (v., pres. pl.) *ride*
ryng (v.) *reign, continue* (**ryngis**, pres. 3rd pers. sing.; **ryngand**, pres. part.; **rang**, p.t.)

save (prep.) *except*
sair, sare (adj.) *bitter, adverse*
sall (v.) *shall, will*
samyn, sammyn (adv.) *together*
saw (n.) *utterance, expressed opinion*

138

schane, schone (v., p.t.) *shone*
scharpe (adj.) *keen, lively*
schaw (v.) *show, express* (**schew**, p.t.)
sche, scho (pron.) *she*
schynand (pres. part.) *shining*
se (v.) *see* (**sene**, inf.; **seyng**, pres. 3rd pers. pl.)
seir, sere (adj.) *many, diverse*
sell, selvyn (pron.) *self, selves*
sen (conj.) *since*
send (v., p.t., p.p.) *sent*
sene (see **se**)
sentence (n.) *judgment, concept*
sere *many, various*

sic, sich, sik (adj., pron.) *such*
syne (adv.) *then*
slychtis (n., pl.) *stratagems*
slyd, slyde (adj.) *slippery*
sore (adv.) *extremely*
spak (v., p.t.) *spoke*
spreit, sprete (n.) *spirit* (**spretis**, pl.)
steid (n.) *place*
stele (v.) *steal* (**stall**, p.t.)
sternys, sterris (n., pl.) *stars*
stok (n.) *tree-stump, wooden stand*
strake (v., p.t.) *struck, crashed*
subtile, suttell, suttyl (adj.) *cunning, skilfully made*
subtelle (adv.) *skilfully, cunningly*
sute (n.) *array, kind*
suyth (n.) *truth*
sum (adj., pron.) *some, someone*
supple (n.) *assistance, support*
sua, swa (adv.) *so*
suyth, swyth (adv.) *quickly*
swage (v.) *diminish, grow calm*

tak (v.) *take* (**tuke**, p.t.; **tane, tone**, p.p.)
tald (v., p.t.) *told, noted*
tha, tho (adj.) *those*
thay (pron.) *they*
thaim (pron.) *them*
thair (adj.) *their*
thair (adv.) *there*
than (adv.) *then*
the (pron.) *thee*
thynk (v.) *think* (see **me thynk**)
thir (adj., pron.) *these*
tho (adv.) *then*
thocht (conj.) *although*
thoill (v.) *suffer* (**tholyt**, p.t.)
thow (pron.) *thou*
thrang (n.) *crowd, trouble*
till (prep.) *to* (see **in tyl**)
till wail, to wale *in abundance*
tyne (v.) *lose* (**tynt**, p.p.)
tyte (adv.) *quickly, at once*
tofore (adv.) *before*
traist (adj.) *loyal*
traist (v.) *trust, expect*
translat, translatit (v., p.p.) *turned, altered*
travail, travel (n.) *labor*
trew (adj.) *steadfast, honest*
twychand (pres. part.) *concerning*
twa (adj.) *two*

uneth (adv.) *hardly*

vary, veray (v.) *lose (one's) wits*
variant (adj.) *variegated, changeable*
vertuus (adj.) *virtuous, powerful*
vysy, vissy (v.) *look about, view* (**vissyand**, pres. part.; **vissyte**, p.p.

139

vyncus (v.) *vanquish* (**vincussyt**, p.t.)

wail, wale (n.) *see* **till wail, to wale**
wake (adj.) *weak*
wally (adj.) *tempestuous*
wary (v.) *curse*; **wareit, waryit** (p.p.)
  accursed
was, wes (v., pl. p.t.) *were*
wate, wote (see **wit**)
weil, wele (adv.) *well, fortunate*
weir, were (n.) *peril, fear*
welth (n.) *prosperity, happiness*
werd (n.) *fate* (**weirdes**, pl.)
wycht (n.) *person*
wirk (v.) *work, cause, make* (**wyrkes**,
  pres. 3rd pers. pl.; **wrocht**, p.t., p.p.)
wit (v.) *know* (**wate, wote**, pres. 3rd
  pers. sing.; **wyst**, p.t.)
wod, wode (n.) *wood, forest*
wone (n.) *dwelling*
worschyp (n.) *honor*
worth (v.) *befall* (**wordyn**, p.p.),
  become
wox (v., p.t.) *grew*
wrate (v., p.t.) *wrote*

ya, yys (interj.) *yes*
yeid (p.t. of go) *went*
yyt (adv.) *yet*
yon, yone (adj., pron.) *that*